D0462810

"Whose beloved are You?"
I asked,
"You who are so
unbearably beautiful?"
"My own," He replied,
"for I am one and alone
love, lover, and beloved
mirror, beauty, eye."[1]

Fakhruddīn 'Irāqī

Fragments of a Love Story

Fragments
of a Love
Story

REFLECTIONS ON
THE LIFE OF A MYSTIC

Llewellyn Vaughan-Lee

THE GOLDEN SUFI CENTER

First published in the United States in 2011 by
The Golden Sufi Center
P.O. Box 456
Point Reyes, California 94956.
www.goldensufi.org

Printed and bound by Thomson-Shore.

ISBN 13: 978-1-890350-34-5
ISBN 10: 1-890350-34-6

Library of Congress Cataloging-in-Publication Data

Vaughan-Lee, Llewellyn.
  Fragments of a love story : reflections on the life of a mystic /
by Llewellyn Vaughan-Lee.
      p. cm.
  Includes bibliographical references and index.
  ISBN 978-1-890350-34-5 (hardcover : alk. paper)
  1. Vaughan-Lee, Llewellyn. 2. Sufis--Biography. 3. Spiritual life.
I. Title.
  BP80.V39V38 2011
  297.4092--dc23
                        2011016448

 This book is printed on 100% post-consumer recycled paper,
     FSC Certified, and processed without chlorine.

Contents

Introduction

THE MYSTICAL PATH is the most difficult, demanding, dangerous, and intoxicating journey one can ever make. It takes one into the depths of the heart, into the abyss and endless love that one finds there. It leads you from the known to the unknown, and then further, into the unknowable, into a darkness brighter than any light. Nothing can prepare you for the heart's journey, for the places it can take you, the depths and heights that are within you. So many times you think you are crazy, bewildered and lost. There are few signposts, often little sense of direction. And yet over the centuries mystics have mapped out the stages of this journey, this opening of the heart. Sufis have written about the chambers of the heart, and how they lead from the pain of separation back to the oneness that is the very nature of love. For the traveler it can be a great relief to know this journey has been mapped, that one is following in the footsteps of those who have gone before. And yet it is also our own unique journey, our heart that is being broken by love, our own sorrow and bliss. It is called the journey "from the alone to the Alone," because we are left alone with the cry of our heart and the places it takes us, both terrible and beautiful—places where there are no books or stories, no words to comfort us, except the story of our own heart, our own confusion, longing and love.

I have been taken along the traditional path of the Sufi that leads from separation back to union, where one discovers the illusory nature of the ego and awakens to the simple and fundamental truth that there is nothing other than God.[2] We are always with God, and even the idea of the path is an illusion: there is nowhere to go, nothing to realize, because everything is God. And this has constellated in me a fundamental question: if everything is God, who is the "I" who has made the journey from separation back to union?

This simple knowing that it is all One, and that the "I" is just an illusion, a veil of separation, has made me question the nature of the very human drama that is played out with our longing and need for God. How much of "our story" is "God's story," and does anything actually belong to us? Is the very idea of our own journey, our story, just a figment of our imagination, a desire to hide the truth of our non-existence, of the emptiness that is always haunting us? And does it matter? When a mother cries for her child her tears are real; when the lover is torn apart by longing his heartache is real. And when we glimpse the light that is all around us the joy is also real.

So what is this love story that unfolds within the heart of the mystic? What is the real nature of a lover's journey back to God? What belongs to the lover, what is our story, and what belongs to the Beloved? Or is it all just one story, One Light split into so many fragments, yet always remaining One Light?

*　　　　　　*　　　　　　*

In the whole of the universe there is only one love story, that of lover and Beloved. And yet this one story is lived in millions of ways, each story a unique fragrance of love. Every cell in creation lives its own love story, its longing for the Source. Human beings have the capacity to make this story conscious, to know the nature of their hidden loving.

This love story is what gives meaning to us all. For many people it is just a dull pulse in the background of their lives, an unconscious sense that there is something more than the surface play of events. But some are drawn into the depths of this love affair, this knowing of love. Their heart and soul are caught in its pull such that their whole life, their whole being, becomes an offering of love.

For most of those souls who are caught in this intoxicating curse of love their story is their own secret—a love affair too intimate to be shared with others. Sometimes even our own mind and ego do not know the depths of our passion, how we are living this calling. When I was sixteen I was awakened to a longing and desire for Truth whose real nature I did not know for many years. Only gradually did I come to consciously know more about this crazy passion—how it was unfolding within me, and how it belonged to an ancient tradition of mystical love. And yet I still kept my own experiences to myself. They belonged to my own intimate relationship within my heart.

Then one afternoon a few years before she died, my teacher told me that I should make my writing and lecturing more personal, should include more of my own story. Up till then I had been reluctant to speak of myself, knowing that it is the "I" that stands between us and the Truth, between lover and Beloved. I had felt stamped inside of me the words of al-Hallāj, "Oh God, through Thy mercy lift this 'it is I' from between us both." But after talking with my teacher I understood the need to also include this "it is I," to tell its story of the journey. And so I wrote a spiritual autobiography, beginning with the morning in the London subway when a paradoxical Zen saying[3] opened within me a door to the light that was all around, to the joy and laughter of what is Real. That story ended almost thirty years later, when amidst the charred hillside of a fire-ravaged California landscape I awoke one morning with the words, "He who was lost has come Home."

Of course that was not the end of the journey. When Dhū'l-Nūn stood on the shore and asked "What is the end of love?" he was told, "Love has no end, because the Beloved has no end." The journey of love is endless. It changes, sometimes as the seasons change, and sometimes as an earthquake alters the landscape irrevocably. And of course, our perception of the journey changes, the way we see this infinite unfolding. Last year when my autobiography[4] was being reprinted, I tried to write an epilogue, to describe how the journey had been over the ten years since I had written this story. And I found that my perception of the whole journey was so different that now I would have written a completely different book. I no longer saw the journey so much through the eyes of the fragmented self who had struggled and aspired, who had made this journey of transformation; I saw it now from the sense of something deeper, more enduring, coming into consciousness within myself.

As I saw how much my perception of the journey had changed I meditated deeply on the question of "who makes the journey?" What is the relationship of the "I" to this Greater Whole that is uncovered even as It is always all around us? There is a journey—we know this because our feet have been made bloody and our hearts have cried so many tears. And yet how can there be a journey when there is only the One and nothing else exists? Is the nature of all of this struggle, the chaos and confusion, just patterns of resistance, a game of shadows played out on a stage that does not really exist? There can only ever be one story that is told, because there is only one Beloved, and yet we are a part of this story; our little "I" must also be a part of the Beloved.

*   *   *

The pieces that follow, written over the years at different times, in different states of mind, are an attempt to articulate this paradox. They are just continuing footsteps on a journey, even as I know there is really no journey. Some appear more personal, more heartfelt, full of the contradictions and difficulties I have experienced. Some are more objective, more detached, often pointing to a larger context for my own experiences. These two types of writing are quite different, and yet for me are like an in-breath and an out-breath, an expression of deep and personal feelings, and then a stepping back to recognize the impersonal nature of the path, remembering that it is "not about me," but a larger story—an ocean in which my own experiences are just a small ripple. But whether intimate and often ambiguous, or more clear and detached, they are all just fragments of a love story, an attempt to articulate this strange mystery of the heart's awakening.

All of these passages circle around what for me is the greatest contradiction, the relationship between the human and the Divine. What within us belongs to God, is an expression of the Divine, and what is just our own human self, this illusory "I" that is finally dissolved by love, the drop that returns to the ocean? When we are caught in the consciousness of the "I," its story is important. It appears to be the meaning of our life as it struggles, suffers, and experiences fleeting happiness or fulfillment. This is how we define our life, how we tell our story. And yet the mystical journey reveals the deeper truth, the story of the ocean rather than the drop, and how that ocean can come crashing into our life. The mystic aspires to this greater story, to live as part of love's infinite ocean, to finally become that ocean. And yet the journey of the drop back to the ocean is also a human story, as we appear to flow here and there, sometimes nearer, sometimes further, from the ocean to which we are returning. This is the contradiction that has drawn my attention. I would like to fully dismiss the ego that has claimed so much of my life, that is so often a veil that separates me from what I perceive to be a greater truth. But I have come to realize that it has a part to play, a story to tell.

So many times I have asked what is it within me that is separate from God, even when I know that everything is That. Why can I not just allow this unending love to live within me? There are moments in meditation, or even during the day, when the lover dissolves, when there is only divine presence. But always some fragment of an "I" returns, and it is this fragment that wants to tell its story, as much as it wants to make the Beloved's mystery known. These writings are just hints at this story, the love, the pain and confusion that belong to it. I know that the mind cannot know, just as every lover knows how the Beloved's story cannot be fully told in words. But there is a deep desire to tell a little of this continuing tale of love, because maybe it too is part of the story of divine love being made known:

If You are Everything
>   then who are all these people?
And if I am nothing
>   what's all this noise about?
You are Totality,
>   everything is You. Agreed.
Then that which is "other-than-You"—
>   *what is it?*
Oh, indeed I know:
>   Nothing exists but You:
but tell me:
>   Whence this confusion?[5]

1

Dust at His Feet

God, the great Beloved, is neither masculine nor feminine. Yet in the following chapters I occasionally call my Beloved "He," even though I know this Divine Being is beyond masculine and feminine. The reason for this choice of language is that in my earliest experiences this Presence came to me as a piercing love, and my soul was feminine—waiting, wanting, longing, and desiring. It is said that all souls are feminine before God, and that it is this divine receptivity that draws down the grace. In these moments of ecstasy we are impregnated by Divine Love, experiencing in the sensuality of the body as well as the merging of the soul what it means to be taken by love. As a man I can only imagine what it feels like to be a woman impregnated by her beloved, but in these moments of rapture this is the feeling that envelops me. Yes, there are moments of a tenderness and caring love that belong to the feminine, a nurturing love that is like a divine mother, a caress of my heart that can only be called feminine. But just as our first kiss is carried as an imprint of love, so this early experience of the soul imprinted into my consciousness a masculine quality of the Beloved that has remained. Later I came to experience my Beloved in the vast emptiness beyond any form and any definition. Here in the endless ocean of love there is no one present, not even the "I" who is loved. But in times of despair and longing, when my heart cries out to God, it still carries a masculine image, the "He" whom I first knew. Thus, these words, although limited, carry the intimacy and immediacy of my own experience.

Like any journey, the heart's journey Home begins with its first step, which, as Hāfiz describes so simply, is the need for a teacher: "Do not take a step on the path of love without a guide. I have tried a hundred times and failed."[6] I begin this story with the presence of my sheikh, him to whom I belong more than I know. Without his invisible presence there would be no story, no journey. Without his grace nothing is possible. My relationship with my teacher is in every heartbeat, in every step of the way. And yet it is the most paradoxical, the most intimate and impersonal relationship a human being can ever have, a relationship of oneness lived initially in a world of duality. It is a relationship that grinds down the wayfarer until nothing is left, and yet that nothing remains, a piece of dust that carries the fragrance of his courtyard. What belongs to me, to this image of a wayfarer, and what belongs to my sheikh, I will never know. Maybe it is the tears that are mine and the love that is his, the need that is mine and the grace that comes from him. And yet in the merging of the heart that is the essence of this relationship there is at times little distinction. All I can ever really express is the heart's gratitude to have such a relationship born of a love that belongs only to the Beloved.

THE RELATIONSHIP between teacher and disciple is one of the great esoteric secrets of humanity. It is a bond within the heart that takes us from the world of the ego and the mind to the further shores of love. It is made out of the purest substance that exists in this world, the secret substance of divine love. Without this secret substance and the bond of love it creates there would be no journey, no intimate unfolding within the core of our being. We would remain stranded forever in the world of forms and its many attachments.

I met my teacher when I was nineteen, when one evening after a talk on the esoteric dimension of mathematics I was introduced to a white-haired old lady who had been sitting in the chair in front of me during the talk. After she had greeted me she looked at me with her piercing blue eyes and I had the physical sensation of becoming a piece of dust on the floor. Then she turned and walked away. I had no understanding of this experience. I did not even think about it for many years, but every Friday from then on I went to her small room beside the train tracks in North London for meditation and tea and cookies. And in that room and in her presence I felt an authority, a power before which something inside me bowed down. To whom or what this authority belonged I did not question. I only knew I had to do whatever I was told.

I had always been a rebellious teenager, never accepting any imposed authority, but here was something so completely different that my mind did not register any doubt or protest. It was as it had always been.

Years later she told me that she was not really my teacher, that when I arrived she had been told in meditation by her teacher, the Sufi master she referred to as Bhai Sahib, that "he would look after me."[7] He had died seven years before I met her, but in the Sufi tradition the disciple can have a connection with a teacher who is no longer in the physical body. It is known as an *Uwaysī* connection, and belongs especially to the Naqshbandi path.[8] It was four years before I began to understand some semblance of this inner relationship, and how that initial experience of being a piece of dust on the floor was a foretaste on the path. Some wayfarers are taken to God through the melting of the heart or the pain of longing. I was to be given the ancient training of complete annihilation, in which the disciple becomes "less than the dust at the feet of the sheikh." As I was told years afterwards in a dream, "He was made soft by a very hard system."

There was a period of two years when I was twenty when my sheikh did not let me sleep for more than three hours a night, destroying my patterns of resistance and spiritual arrogance with the simple method of exhaustion. The whole day I longed for sleep, only to be given just a taste of it when I finally went to bed, before an inner energy awoke me. I was living in a small, damp room at the time, and there is nothing more dispiriting than watching the minutes and hours go by in the dark dampness, knowing that another day of constant exhaustion is waiting. I had come to the path with a sense of my own spiritual importance, having had experiences in meditation since I was sixteen. After a few months nothing mattered except the struggle through the day and the longing for sleep.

Then, one hot summer afternoon when I was twenty-three, in the most intense few hours of my life I was confronted by the deepest suffering of my whole being. This suffering was a potent and piercing pain in the heart that drew me inwards, deeper and deeper into an agony hidden in the very core of my being. This anguish, this pure pain, lasted for hours, until in a moment of inner revelation my sheikh made me conscious on the level of the soul. I knew I was a soul, not just an ego, and I was with my sheikh in a way I had never known before. The link of love on the level of the soul was made conscious, never to be lost again.

Gradually, over the following years, I became aware of the depths of my belonging to him, that I am here to serve him, that I have been trained to do his bidding. He guided me from the inner world with kindness and severity. Once, when my children were young and I was continually tidying the house after them, his voice gently came to me, "You don't have to keep tidying up!" While on another occasion, when I was suffering intensely from *kundalini*, Mrs. Tweedie went into meditation and asked Bhai Sahib if he could help me. His response was simply, "He can bear it."

My relationship with my sheikh is one of total subservience and love, a recognition that nothing matters in this world except to do his work and to please him. I came to know him as an inner presence, someone I could turn to in meditation and prayer, whose help would be present when I needed it most. And yet often over the years he seemed to leave me alone to struggle with my difficulties and make mistakes. I have experienced the devastation of emptiness and desolation when this connection was veiled, and real anguish when I displeased him, when I felt that I had failed my sheikh. But I have come to know that this relationship is the one thread of love that this world cannot break, because it is made of a different substance that is stronger than all the difficulties of this world. It belongs to the ancient secret of love and devotion, a belonging so primal that it is before creation. It is part of the substance of my soul and gives meaning to every moment of every day. When I was thirty-six and was sent to America to lecture on Sufism, although I had never lectured before, in a vision I was given the simple message, "The grace of your guru is in your heart. This is all you need to know." That message, that imprint within the heart, was all I needed. And later, when I gave a talk in a trailer in a car park at a New Age Expo in San Francisco, and his grace and presence were so tangible that everyone could feel it, I just inwardly bowed down in awe.

Held by this thread of love, this connection from heart to heart, I was given a love that is so complete that every cell of the body was fulfilled and I knew the bliss of the soul. This was not an abstract, imagined happening, but something so concrete that I can still remember that first time, when lying in meditation I felt a love like butterfly wings on the edge of my heart. I had been brought up without much love, sent to boarding school at the age of seven, and suddenly here was a love that filled me from within, that brought me alive in ways that I did not believe possible. And in this love I felt and knew his touch.

Through this invisible presence I was taken from the world of duality back to the oneness of the heart, and further, into the dimensions of non-being, the emptiness that is the real home of the mystic. I was shown the infinite inner spaces where love is born, and a quality of consciousness that belongs to light upon light. In the ancient tradition, I was destroyed and remade, so that I could be of service to my sheikh and the Beloved. When I first came to the path I was arrogant and also fractured, almost broken apart by a longing I could not contain, by an intensity for spiritual life that had no place in my middle-class world. But unknowingly I was taken in hand by a great master who put me back together and taught me humility and the simplicity of real service. He opened my heart and awoke me to a realization of the oneness of life that is all around us. And he guided me, with humor, patience, and love, knowing my faults and accepting me.

Through this relationship I have also come to know the real power that belongs to God and those who are in service to God. In our outer life we often seem surrounded by power dynamics, played out in the family or the workplace. We also see the corruptive power dynamics on the world stage. But in the relationship with a real teacher, one who is merged into the Absolute, who is one with God, there is a power of a completely different magnitude, a power that belongs to the Creator and not the creation. This is a power that wants nothing for itself but just *is*. It has been hidden from the world for many centuries. When I experience this power inwardly, when in deep meditation I feel in the presence of my sheikh, my whole being trembles and bows down. When people talk of power dynamics with spiritual teachers something in me laughs, because they have never known what real spiritual power is. The disciple does not argue or doubt before such pure energy. The only response is awe and submission.

Each of us can tell many stories about our relationship with our teacher. Some of these are painful, humiliating, or humorous. There are also all the dramas of projection, in which we cover the real nature of this soul relationship with the patterns of conditioning, with the images and fantasies of our personality. We try to place our teacher within the sphere of our own psyche, often creating difficulties through which we suffer and hopefully learn. And then there are the most precious moments, when through the grace of the guru we are given an awareness of the nature of the divine, within ourselves and within life, when we glimpse the wonder of what is real.

Because I never knew my sheikh in physical form I escaped many of the dramas of projection that I see others suffer through. I never tried to limit his love with the demands of my personal psyche, my need for love and acceptance, or my patterns of rejection. Yet I can also see how this drama of projection is part of the uncovering of the soul, part of the way we come closer to the real love that is in the core of our being. We come to recognize that the teacher's love for us was complete at the beginning, was the one truth in a world of illusion. A true teacher allows his disciples to create all the dramas they desire, to follow the paths of their imagining, knowing that the real love that is given from heart to heart will make itself known despite all the obstacles the disciple may place in its path.

For many years in my inner experiences he appeared detached and hard, rarely showing the love I later came to know. Now I have come to know how one of the greatest dangers of this tremendous love and closeness is a psychological and even emotional dependence that constricts rather than frees the wayfarer. He is my teacher, not the loving parent I never had, and he forced me to stand on my own feet. Only later, in moments of sweetest tenderness, did I consciously experience the love that has always been there.

It was in those terrible times when everything seemed to be lost, when the curtains of the world closed so tightly around me, and I wondered how I could take another step on a path that seemed to have betrayed me, that the love appeared, that presence was felt. It is so simple and ordinary, this love that binds me to my sheikh, this knowing that I belong to him. Nothing else matters. In that closed circle there is only his love, his kindness, his understanding. Once, in a time of extreme despair, when I seemed to be thrown against the wall, when everything seemed to be lost, I realized that in the bond between us there was only oneness and that if I trusted him completely, then he must trust me completely. Then nothing else mattered—there was nowhere else to go.

He has taken me from place to place in the inner world, opened doors within my heart and soul that would otherwise have remained closed, reminded me of my real nature. And he has put up with my endless complaints, my tears and despair, even my anger at how I feel I am treated! He can see the bigger picture and sometimes will tell me about an insurmountable problem, "It will pass." Or he points out where I need to be more attentive, where the work needs greater care, or even where I need to be less concerned. And always underneath there is this quality of love without which I could not breathe, could not move, could not meditate or pray. Even when I feel so alone, so forgotten, I know in my depths that he is part of me, I am part of him.

This love is a bond of belonging that we bring into the world. After all of the difficulties, perseverance, and joy that belong to the path, this belonging remains, an axis of truth that is not an abstract idea but a lived reality. The beginning of the path is an awakening to this inner core of love, and the journey makes it real in this world, until you come to realize that it is always present. Over the years I discovered my relationship with my sheikh as a quality of belonging that is total and absolute, in which I would give everything again and again. And it is also a quality of pure freedom in which one bows down only before God.

My sheikh said that the only real love in this world is between teacher and disciple.[9] All other forms of love are an illusion. The love between teacher and disciple is stamped with the name of God, the same name that is written into the heart of the disciple. We are given this love at the beginning of the journey. Without it there could be no path, no stages of the journey, no awakening. This love uncovers what is real within our heart and takes us beyond the world of appearances into the courtyard of our sheikh. Here we discover the sweet fragrance that was always present, the fragrance of a soul that belongs to God. And, in the words of a Persian poem, if people ask, "Why are you so fragrant?"

> I am a dust people tread upon,
> But I partake of the fragrance of the
>   courtyard of a Saint.
> It is not me,
>   I am just ordinary dust.[10]

2

Chambers of the Heart

The following chapter comes from a talk that was first given in October 2008. It was a talk that I had wanted to give for a long time, even though, as is often the way of things, I only understood afterward why I had wanted to give it. It was as if I could not continue onward until I had given this talk, which is a very personal statement about the path. It was a talk about the Sufi teachings on the latā'if, *the spiritual chambers within the heart. But, as it is also based upon my own inner experiences, I discovered that it was the story of my own journey, my own traveling within the heart.*

My mystical path has taken me through these openings within the heart. This is the traditional Sufi journey, and yet it is also individual for each of us. Different Sufi schools even describe different numbers of latīfah, *of these subtle centers, and they are often given different interpretations. Although we are all making the same journey, from separation to union, we each make it in our own unique way. The Sufi says "there are as many ways to God as there are human beings, as many as the breaths of the children of men." And yet there are also signposts for this journey, stages we each travel through. In my own journey it has given me great solace to discover this map that has been drawn and re-drawn by those who have gone before. Although in my love and longing I am alone, I am also in the company of others. There is a path, though we each walk it in our own way, make it bloody with our own footsteps.*

And yet, paradoxically, although it is our own blood, our own footsteps, the journey itself takes us to the annihilation of the "I." The experience of the oneness of God brings the realization that there is no separate "I" to have made this journey, and in the deepest sense, no journey. Then in the next chamber of the heart is the experience of the nothingness which underlies all of creation, and we are that nothingness. This is the abyss which is waiting for each of us, the intoxicating darkness of complete extinction. Who then remains to tell any story? And beyond even this nothingness is the Absolute Truth of God.

... he has seen, with His help,
what was concealed from his eyes.
The meanings of things were revealed to him ...

al-Hakīm at-Tirmidhī[11]

THE JOURNEY HOME

The Sufi path is a journey Home, a journey from the outer world of illusions to the inner reality that belongs within the heart. This is a journey of transformation that takes the wayfarer out of his subjective dream-state, so that he can fulfill his divine destiny. For the wayfarer, the journey Home happens within the heart:

> Be an external resident and let your heart travel,
> Travelling without legs is the best kind of travel.[12]

On this journey within the heart the Sufi travels from the outer world of the creation to the inner world of the Creator, where love unveils the secret nature of the human being, our divine heritage.

We are drawn towards the path in order to make this inner journey, the journey back to God, from separation to union. The heart is the locus of our divine nature and the journey within the heart unveils this secret, what is known as the "secret of secrets." One of the greatest paradoxes of human existence is that we are veiled from our divine nature, our innermost union with God. Most people live solely in the physical, emotional, mental dimension of the outer world of the senses. This is the apparent existence in which they live and die, the dream-state that is called life. The Sufi refers to this apparent reality as the world of creation, in contrast to the spiritual truth of the world of the Creator. The world of the Creator is our spiritual heritage, the direct experience of our divine nature.

The real secret of human existence is this inner reality beyond the world of the senses. Just as we have a physical body, we have a spiritual body that exists in this inner world. This spiritual body is made of light, and functions as a living spiritual organism. Just as we use our physical body to travel in the outer world, with our spiritual body we can travel and experience the inner worlds. Also, just as we have two eyes to see the outer world, we have a single eye of the heart that can see the world of divine truth. Since the very beginning human beings have been given spiritual practices to gain access to this reality, to uncover this secret. Meditation, *dhikr* or mantras, breathing practices and other spiritual techniques have been developed to help the practitioner make the transition from the outer world to a direct inner experience of their spiritual nature. Sufi esoteric teaching is based on the understanding that one of the most direct ways to access this inner truth is through the spiritual center of the heart. The heart is the organ of our divine consciousness. The secret of our divine nature is placed within the heart, and through the heart we can experience its reality:

> God said through the Holy Prophet, "Man is My secret and I am his secret. The inner knowledge of the spiritual essence is a secret of My secrets. Only I put this into the heart of My good servant, and none may know his state other than Me."[13]

Sufism developed an esoteric science of the spiritual nature of the heart. Early Sufis uncovered the truth that there are subtle spiritual centers or subtle bodies (latīfah, plural latā'if) within the physical body. They located five subtle centers—our lower nature (nafs) and the four elements—in the world of creation. Within the heart they described five[14] subtle centers that belong to our spiritual body. It is through these latā'if located within the heart, these "chambers of the heart," that one makes the journey Home. Each latīfah also represents a different subtle body enabling the wayfarer to experience and travel in a different inner spiritual realm.

Each of the latā'if belongs to a particular stage of the journey. One can journey within the latā'if in the heart into deeper and deeper states of spiritual truth, deeper levels of reality. And although this is an individual journey, unique to each wayfarer, each of these chambers has a specific spiritual quality. The chambers of the heart are thus a map of the journey.

THE HEART, QALB

The first, outermost chamber is called the Heart, Qalb. It is described as active and is associated with love and longing. Its color is yellow. The journey Home begins with the awakening of longing within the heart, the longing to return back to God. The soul's primal cry of separation ignites our secret passion for union with God. This great love affair begins with this cry, a love affair that will tear apart every thread of our being and draw us from the separation of the ego to the union of the Self. For some it begins quietly, with a strange feeling of discontent or dissatisfaction. We want something else, not present in our lives; nothing seems quite right, nothing fulfills us. We do not realize that we have embarked on the great journey of the soul, the love affair with the great Beloved—that we are being subtly poisoned by love.

For others this pain of longing is awakened more dramatically, perhaps in meeting a teacher, as in the words of a Persian poem,

> "The world is full of beautiful things until an old man with a beard came into my life and set my heart aflame with longing and made it pregnant with Love. How can I look at the loveliness around me, how can I see it, if it hides the Face of my Lover?"[15]

When Rūmī met Shams in the marketplace, his heart's burning began, and his world was destroyed and remade by love. As Rūmī said, "It is burning of the heart I want. This burning which is everything. More precious than a worldly empire because it calls God secretly in the night." Through this awakening love we are turned away from the world and back to God. Our heart calls out in love and longing, and the passion of the soul begins to unfold within us. All that matters is this love affair, and the tears we cry are its tribute.

Our heart has been awakened to its memory of being together with God, with that primal mystery that is at the root of all that is. What is simpler than to give the lover a taste of this sweet intimate love, a love that touches every cell in the body and the substance of the soul—and then to withdraw, leaving the lover alone, more desolate than anything she knew before? Love calls to us through the pain of our longing.

This is the most tender, terrible and beautiful love affair. And it is a secret, hidden from the outer world, from your friends and even your partner. It belongs to the inside of your heart, to the fabric of the soul. And what is there to say? What words can convey the sweet bitterness of real longing? To quote Abū Sa'īd,

"My secret will be a secret," the Friend said.
"Your bloodied shirt no one will see,
   when the heart bleeds.
No one will wake with your moan late at night,
the smoke from your heart, burning in this fire,
   no one will detect."[16]

In the night we lie awake, crying and calling to God, to our Beloved. We have tasted one sip of the wine of divine love and become lost, wanting nothing but another sip. We have become addicted to love, a slave of love. And this is no idealized love affair, but a real pain that grips the heart. The heart bleeds with longing and desire, and the tears one cries are the only evidence of this primal pain. When my teacher came back from being with her sheikh she kept a white handkerchief as a memento. Before she met him it had been blue, but had become bleached white with all the tears she cried.

To someone who has not tasted this sweet poison no words can convey its power, passionate and painful. This is a love that destroys and burns as much as it brings bliss and infinite sweetness. It is a love affair of paradoxes, of intoxicating intimacy and terrible loneliness. As Rūmī writes:

> "The Beloved is so sweet, so sweet," they repeat;
> I show them the scars where His polo-stick
>   thrashed me.
> "The Beloved is terrible, a maniac," they wail;
> I show them my eyes, melting in
>   His tender passion.[17]

We are beaten by love in the cruelest way, made vulnerable by its sweet pain, tenderized by longing. Sometimes the aloneness seems more than we can bear, as our primal hunger for this love makes us destitute. How long must we wait for our Beloved? How can we live in a world without His tender touch? Will our tears draw Him back? Do our cries reach Him? And then His love is suddenly present, and everything in us melts, and every pain, every tear is forgotten. And this sweetness can last for a moment, for an hour, for a day. And then once again He withdraws, and we are alone again, more desperate than before, and we wonder, how much can one bear? How can my Beloved torture me with His absence?

This state of love and longing lasts for years. It is more intimate and more desolate than anything one can imagine. With every other relationship you have barriers that protect you, patterns of protection. But this love affair happens in the fabric of your own heart. To quote the great lover al-Hallāj:

> You run between the heart and its sheath
> As tears run from the eyelids.[18]

And this is just the outermost chamber of the heart, just the beginning of the journey.

The awakening of love and longing that marks the beginning of the journey is a very dynamic, even turbulent experience. It is a love that burns and purifies, cleansing the heart of many impurities that belong to the ego and *nafs*, the desires and distortions in which the pure soul of the newborn child becomes trapped as it grows into the density of this world. The fire in the heart begins to burn away this dross, often confronting us with our own darkness, our shadow qualities. Then, when we have lived and bled with our longing, and enough of our darkness and impurities have been burned away, a space within us opens that belongs to Spirit.

SPIRIT, *RUH*

The second chamber of the heart is called Spirit, *Ruh*. Its color is red. In contrast to the active attribute of the first chamber, Spirit has a quality of quietude and tranquility. Here a certain light within us becomes accessible, a light that has this quality of tranquility, peace and quietude. This light within the heart belongs to God. The longing of the heart also belongs to God in its essential nature; it is His longing for Himself that burns within us. But we experience it as *our* longing, *our* pain of separation, *our* passion. We want something, we want the Truth or God. Our longing is close to the physical world; it is sometimes even accompanied by a physical pain in the heart, as well as by fear—for example a fear of abandonment and other emotions arising from our lower nature. The light of the Spirit is very different and comes to us only after longing has purified us.

When we cry to God, the light of our longing attracts another light, the light of Spirit. To quote Najm al-Dīn Kubrā:

> There are lights which ascend and lights which descend. The ascending lights are the lights of the heart; the descending lights are those of the Throne. Creatural being [the lower-self, the ego] is the veil between the Throne and the heart. When this veil is rent and a door to the Throne opens in the heart, like springs toward like. Light rises toward light and light comes down upon light, *"and it is light upon light"*....
> (Qur'an 24:35)[19]

Our longing, the cry of our heart, both breaks through the veil of the ego and draws down the light that belongs to our divine nature. This second chamber is the place where the two lights, the two worlds, meet, where we are taken into the real mystery of our divine nature, of the part of our self that belongs to God. That is why we first have to suffer the pain of purification. Otherwise we would pollute this light with our darkness and desires. It would become distorted, contaminated by our impurities.

In the chamber of Spirit the miracle of divine birth begins to take place, and it is always unexpected, coming in stillness and silence. Irina Tweedie describes how she first experienced it:

> And so it came... it tiptoed itself into my heart, silently, imperceptibly, and I looked at it with wonder. It was still small, a light-blue flame, trembling softly. It had the infinite sweetness of a first love, like an offering of fragrant flowers with gentle hands, the heart full of stillness and wonder and peace.[20]

After the inner dramas and tears and sleepless nights, suddenly something else is present, coming with a quality of peace and tranquility, or quietude. It is really our first true experience of our divine nature, of what belongs to the Self whose core is peace. Something within us is now at peace. We have found this divine light, the Spirit within us, and our soul is at rest:

> O soul at rest, return to thy Lord, well pleased and well pleasing. Enter as My servant, enter into My heaven. (Qur'an 89:27-30)

We have been given a taste of what is eternal and essential, and nothing can take it away because it does not belong to this world. This is the beginning of the transition from effort to effortlessness, as this Spirit now begins to work on you from within. Whatever happens in our life and on our journey, this light and its tranquility remain. It may be hidden under the surface but it is always present because it belongs to God.

MYSTERY, *SIRR*

The Spirit opens us to the third chamber of the heart, Mystery, *Sirr*. Its color is white and it belongs to intimacy with God. *Sirr* also means secret, and for the Sufis the greatest secret of creation is that we are one with God. In the chamber of *Sirr* you experience this secret inwardly and outwardly. Within your heart you are merged into the oneness of God in which there is nothing other than God. The duality of lover and Beloved has dissolved to reveal love's deeper truth:

> "Whose beloved are You?"
>   I asked,
> "You who are so
>   unbearably beautiful?"
> "My own," He replied,
>   "for I am one and alone
> love, lover, and beloved
>   mirror, beauty, eye."[21]

Our Beloved whom we have longed for is in our heart in such intimacy that there are no longer two, but one. We are with our Beloved in complete oneness. This is when the love affair becomes fulfilled, a fulfillment that is tangible, that lives inside of us with every breath—it is intimate, it is oneness, and it is love. It is so tender; He is our friend, our companion, our lover, and He is always with us. Even when we are left alone He is with us. It is a meeting, a merging of lovers such as we long for in sexual union, in which we forget our self completely: we die and are dissolved in love. And yet the intensity and sweetness of this inner meeting make sexual intimacy seem shallow. It is not a meeting of bodies, but a merging within the heart, within the substance of our own soul.

There is a price to be paid for this experience of union, which the Sufis call the process of *fanā*, the annihilation of the ego. The ego defines our sense of being separate, the "I," and mystics have long known that in order to reclaim our true oneness and divine nature the ego has to bow down and relinquish its control. It is the ego that separates lover and Beloved, as al-Hallāj affirms:

> Between me and You there lingers an "it is I"
> > which torments me...
> Ah! lift through mercy this "it is I!" from
> > between us both![22]

The price of love is our own self, which we pay with our tears and suffering. When you are going through it, you wonder how long you can last, how you can survive this endless longing, the bleeding, the pain, as the "I" is being torn apart by love. And then one day you notice that the pain has gone, and instead there is an intimacy, a secret meeting, a deep knowing that you are with your Beloved. And you remember—you look in your diary, in your dream journal, and you say, oh yes, I remember those days, but how could I ever be separate from Him

whom I love, Him to whom I belong? There is only oneness, and this oneness was always there. In the words
of 'Attār: "Your image is in my eyes, Your name is in my
mouth, Your dwelling place is in my breast. How could
You be remote from me?"[23]

This meeting of lovers is so sweet. And as with any
love affair you always remember the *first* kiss because it
is so unexpected, so tender. I remember for myself: one
afternoon when I was about twenty-nine, I was lying in
meditation, and suddenly there were butterfly wings on
the edge of my heart and the sweetness was almost un-
bearable, a sweetness that went through every cell of the
body, every fiber of my being. And this was just a little
touch of this intimacy, a little touch of this closeness—a
taste of this extraordinary secret that we are one with
God. And there was a completeness in this meeting that
is difficult to describe, a completeness that comes with
the knowing that only this oneness is real, and that all
the feelings of separation are like mist burned away by
the morning sun.

Sufis say that until you swim in the ocean of unity
you are not a real Sufi; you are just a traveler on the road
of intent. You are *on your way* to being a Sufi. Only when
this mystery has been awakened within you does the real
transformation begin, not the transformation of the ego,
but the transformation of the soul as it becomes infused
with the deep knowing of the oneness of God. And this
secret is a gift.[24] With all of your efforts, your strivings,
your longing and devotion, you could not find it. But when
you are ready you are taken into this embrace, into this
chamber within the heart. He whom you love takes you
back to Himself, back to the primal oneness that belongs

to every cell of creation. And it is a meeting of lovers, a merging into oneness, that gets deeper and deeper, more and more intoxicating, more and more complete. To quote the martyr of love's unity, al-Hallāj, "I have become the One I love, and the One I love has become me!"[25]

This mystery of oneness that is given within the heart awakens us to the oneness that is all around. We begin to see the outer world with the intimacy of lovers and the eyes of oneness:

If you dwell with the Friend
In genuine intimacy,
Then, in the whole world,
You will see the incomparable God.
Since the whole world
Is the living mirror of God,
It is impossible to see anything
Aside from God.[26]

What happens is that the oneness within the heart is reflected in the outer world. The world becomes another meeting place with God, another aspect of oneness. We begin to feel His presence and see His face in the world: "Wheresoever you turn, there is the face of God."[27] This love affair within the heart begins to get played out in the outer world, which, no longer a place that denies God, becomes a place in which we come to know our Beloved in different ways. Life and the outer world begin to reveal their secret face as a revelation of God. The mystic says that God in His Essence is unknowable, but one can come to know Him through His creation. His oneness is all around us. It is all God:

Rose and mirror and sun and moon—
>   what are they?
Wherever we looked,
>   there was always Thy face.[28]

The book of creation is a story of oneness revealed in so many forms, every form reflecting the Creator in a unique way. The chamber of *Sirr* opens us to this wonder. Through the world's many images we come to know God, His light and His darkness, His beauty and His terror. We learn not to judge but to witness His presence, even in a world that has forgotten Him. And even this forgetfulness belongs to God.

Oneness is always all around us, and yet until this chamber of the heart is opened, it is veiled from our consciousness. The ninth-century Sufi, al-Hakīm at-Tirmidhī, one of the earliest Sufis to write about the chambers of the heart, observes that there are lights within the heart with which we can see and know what is true. These lights are veiled by the darkness of forgetfulness, but they are always present. And in this chamber, which at-Tirmidhī refers to as "innermost," is the light of unification with which one can see the oneness of God in the inner and outer worlds. Only with this light of divine oneness can one perceive the true meaning of things, contemplate the divine truth within creation.

For the Sufi the deepest purpose of creation is the divine revelation of God to Himself, "I was a hidden treasure and I longed to be known, so I created the world."[29] Through seeing God in His creation we participate in this mystery of His coming to know Himself in His world:

He had but one purpose in bringing forth both worlds' Existence. To see Himself in the mirror of the soul and then to become the lover of Himself who is without flaw.[30]

The heart of the lover is a place of divine revelation of the Beloved. This is the deepest meeting of lover and Beloved, the true affirmation of oneness and the nature of *Sirr*.

When we see with the light of unification we can see the way He is revealing Himself anew in every moment. And we are a part of this revelation. Just as on our own inner journey we realize that the journey is not about us, about our journey back to God, but about our Beloved— that it is His love that is awakened in the heart, His desire for us that draws us back to His Oneness, that, as al-Hallāj affirms, "No, it is You who calls me to Yourself"[31]—as the single eye of the heart opens we begin to experience that the world is also not about us, our struggles and dramas, but about the great Beloved. We begin to awaken in a very different world, a world of things as they really are, without all of our distortions and projections.[32] Through the light of the heart the lover begins to experience the world that belongs to God: we share in God's revelation of divine Oneness.

Through our daily life we live this mystery; we awaken to this consciousness that it is all about the Beloved. We experience how everything is a meeting place of lover and Beloved. And we are allowed to live this because we have paid the price on the altar of love, because we have given our heart for this mystery to be unveiled.

And this is the third chamber of the heart, the chamber of Mystery, the chamber of *Sirr*, the place of divine oneness within the heart and within the consciousness of the world, in which we experience nearness with God and discover our true Self, our divine nature, and through which we are able to see things as they truly are.

ARCANUM, *KHAFĪ*

But then the journey continues. Beyond the chamber of *Sirr* is the Arcanum, *Khafī*, whose color is black and whose qualities are of negation. It is associated with the extinction and absence of self; here all consciousness is dissolved, lost in the inner emptiness. Al-Ansārī describes how through the heart we find and then lose:

> The beginning of contemplation
> > is vision by means of the heart:
> > then comes nearness of the heart;
> > then comes finding by means of the heart,
> then comes direct observation by means of the heart;
> then comes fading of the heart in the Manifest;
> and beyond that nothing can be said.[33]

Earlier in the journey we experienced the painful process of *fanā*, the dying of the ego that is a doorway into the secret of the heart, this death in love through which we awaken into the wonder and light of our divine being, the Self. What is less understood is the deeper extinction that happens to one's very being that takes place in this next chamber of the heart. This is an extinction so total that nothing remains, no sense of Self, no awareness of oneness, nothing. It is like being absorbed into a black hole that takes everything, even your light:

You are a placeless fire
All places burn away in,
A whirlpool of Nowhere
Drowning me deeper, deeper.[34]

In the primal nothingness of non-existence everything is lost. Any trace of the wayfarer is gone. What is there to say about what is gone, except that nothing remains? To quote Abū Sa'īd:

"For many years in every way I've sought a sign (of God). When I saw what I was seeking, I became lost. I became a drop in the ocean. Now I'm lost behind the secret's curtain. The lost person doesn't find again what was lost. Since you've become lost, what can you find of what was lost? Since the road is closed what can you find behind the curtain?"[35]

Yet there is a process to this extinction, a meaning to this annihilation. But this is not for the fainthearted, nor for those who want to abide in the bliss of the Self, to remain in the intimacy of union. Those who have paid the price of *fanā*, who have gone beyond the illusions of the ego and watched every identity be burnt away by longing, can remain in the circle of love, living and witnessing His oneness. But there is a doorway beyond that chamber of the heart. This is the doorway of non-existence, where a cold and brutal wind blows away even the secrets of oneness. Its color is black because it has no color. This primal emptiness has a power and vastness beyond anything that is created, and it destroys everything that ever existed. It is the real home of the mystic, of the one who is "lost in the company of those who are lost in God."

> A mystic is one who passes away
> He abides in the essence of that which is Real.
> Why would one be drawn into
> this nothingness?

Why would one leave behind the intoxication of *Sirr*? Does one have a choice, or is one stamped with the sign of annihilation? This is a state of being with God in the uncreated, in the nothingness before and after creation. It has an inhuman quality, which can initially evoke fear and desolation. Yet in the cold darkness of this inner emptiness there is a completeness that is beyond our comprehension, not the completeness of things coming together, but a vaster wholeness that carries the deep knowing that everything is present in the unknown, a vast and dynamic realm that carries the freedom of non-existence. Putting down the clothes of existence, leaving all semblance of anything created, one leaves all burdens behind, and there is freedom beyond any imaginings.

Initially, as one enters this state, there may, paradoxically, be an awareness of one's non-existence. A fragment of consciousness may remain that gives one a taste of what is meant by extinction. One has the awareness that one is not, and this awareness is the deepest fulfillment, even more complete than divine union. One senses the Reality that is waiting in the emptiness. But then even this awareness is lost as one goes deeper into the emptiness. Nothing remains, and one returns from this inner state with the awareness that one was taken beyond any consciousness. Everything was left behind. When you return to the created world you carry the knowledge of the nothingness that is within and around everything like the dynamic space between the stars and within every atom and every particle. And you sense the power of this nothingness. You know that it is Real.

In this station of the heart there is no longer any journey, any traveler or any path. It is beyond longing, beyond intoxication, beyond even the duality of life and death. What remains after annihilation? And yet this state underlies everything, as Irina Tweedie's sheikh describes with the simple sentence, "There is nothing but Nothingness."[36]

SUPER ARCANUM, *AKHFA*

There is a further mystical state, beyond the complete extinction in the emptiness of God, and this is the deepest mystery, *Akhfa*. It has the quality of comprehensive synthesis, and its color is green. It belongs to annihilation and consummation. For the Sufi green is the color of Absolute Truth. The journey Home is sometimes described as an ascent of the mountain of Qāf at whose summit is an emerald rock where shines the midnight sun. This light is beyond oneness and beyond nothingness. What is there to say of this Ultimate Truth, except that It is at the core of everything that is and is not? And It is completely different from anything you can think or imagine. It is neither like this nor like that. It is the sun of His face, whose single glance destroys everything. There are no words to describe how beautiful and terrible It is. It is unknown and unknowable. And yet It is the Primal Reality and the final stage of the mystical journey:

> God answers Dhū'l-Nūn as to how long He still wishes to kill the men of God, "I kill him… and if he has disappeared completely, then I show him the sun of My face…. When the shadow disappeared in the sun, then he became nothing—and God knows best."[37]

These are the stages of the mystical journey, the chambers of the heart through which the wayfarer travels, discovering the secrets of his spiritual nature. Not everyone makes the whole journey to the final chamber of *Akhfa*. The last two chambers are particularly inaccessible. But within the tradition and within the wayfarer all these chambers are present, in potential, even if they are never lived. They are within the chain of transmission, the link of love that unites the hearts of all those who are drawn to this journey.

While most people live in the external world of the senses, mystics have uncovered an inner reality that is our esoteric nature. The Sufi tradition gives us access to these inner realms through the different chambers of the heart. This is our heritage, given by the grace of the tradition—these stages on the journey within the heart that lead from the awakening of longing to Absolute Truth, as step by step we are taken into these dimensions of light and love and emptiness, uncovering what it really means to be a human being.

3

Words to Myself

A Collection of Short Pieces
Written Over a Decade

Following is a very personal collection of writings, written without being intended for publication. Many were written at times of inner crisis, even despair, as I struggled with myself on this journey of the soul. They were often an attempt to understand what was happening, to bring into consciousness some inner conflict with the hope of reconciling it. They hint at some of my own encounters with the Divine, especially with a primal emptiness into which I have been drawn. This emptiness has drowned me again and again, taken me beyond light and dark into states of non-existence which the "I" then struggles to comprehend.

These writings hint at the love and the intense confusion and pain these experiences often left in their wake, of the unanswerable questions and the occasional glimpses of insight they gave rise to. What is this substance I call myself when there is this overwhelming emptiness, this abyss of non-being? What remains after that experience? How can there be a journey when there is nothing, nowhere to go? What is the relationship between this primal emptiness and the manifest world? How does one live between them, between non-being and being? How can non-being be lived in this world? Can it be lived? Here there are no answers, but the tortuous passion of what has been experienced, of the darkness of Divine love.

I have included them because they give a taste of how the path lived inside me, to what dark and confusing places it often took me, as well as the touches of infinite love it gave me. I do not expect these words to explain these states even to myself, but there was a need to write them, to give some inner context to the love that has drowned me, and how this feels.

I have arranged these writings chronologically with no attempt at any thematic order. They are expressions of the moment, alive with the intensity of that moment in which a certain clarity might come and go. But slowly over the years something emerged, even amid all the pain and confusion, a fragrance of some greater meaning in which even the illusory "I" has its place.

Thoughts

To search is to find what the heart has always known, that there are no boundaries to love. Finding this leaves us frightened, on the edge of our expectations, unaware of the simplicity of the unknown. In silence we become and then unbecome, know and are unknown. For so long we have searched for this emptiness, hoping, expecting, to find something. Is it a realization that we have longed for? Is it a meeting with a lost lover? Always you thought that there was something to seek, a journey to make. Now you stand on the precipice, looking out over the horizon of your self, and you know it is otherwise.

In our own inner emptiness or in our day-by-day existence there is no answer but the end of a question. Here there is no seeking, no lover lost and found. There is no looking, nothing to reach for, no path to follow. But within there is an answer, not in form but in substance. The source brings something beyond the passions of day-to-day life to the surface, something we need to nourish rather than define. There is a bigger wholeness hidden, waiting at the corner of the moments, watching from behind the thoughts.

This wholeness has an unexpected purpose. It is not a bouquet of roses. It is not something lost and found. It is *other*, from across time and beyond space. It has a scent, unidentifiable and yet distinct, like a wine that has been fermented *elsewhere* and retains that quality.

You wait for something to happen, and there is nothing to happen, yet the happening comes closer, like a map that reveals your own garden as an undiscovered place. There is another presence, another pattern, not hidden but unrevealed. There is a tender sense of silence, without prayer to or from. In the moments of our own silence we are welcomed, as both stranger and friend. We need to allow the presence to become present, not in defined moments, but as a flow. The river is here, not hidden behind the bank or across the horizon. The silence, unbidden, is always present. It carries a quality of walled gardens where the roses bloom in abundance. In the tranquility of the moment nothing is defined or captured. This world is infused with the other, steeped with the dew of timelessness.

You thought that prayer was a relationship of you and God, you and the teacher, you and another. You were *so wrong*. Prayer just is. In that *isness* everything is included. You, the Beloved, the object of your prayer, and the will to unfold the eternal into the present, to cross the borders of time and space, saturate the now with eternity. There is no other. You were always alone but you thought it was a state of incompleteness. You waited for someone to come. How can there be another when He is *one*? Is that so terrible that you must run and hide? To whom can you talk when there is no other? To whom can you relate? Fish's eyes glow in the darkness.

Always you waited. If there is a journey, a relationship, there must be a state to strive for, work to help with, a project, a potential. Such a joke. It is not even a good idea. There are no prospects. You are fortunate enough to disbelieve in everything. You are blessed to have no partner—always waiting at the bus stop for the bus that never comes, *because there is nowhere to go.*

The world spins around a place of silence and waiting. You need to enter that silence, and wait in the eternal present in which there is no future. Be present, mirrored into silence, as the waves of non-existence crash against the shores of being. Otherwise for whom do we wait? The days unfold in their own majesty of sunrise and sunset, and we miss that magic moment when non-being comes into existence, sheds its skin of invisibility and begins the dance that some call life. We need to watch out of the corner of our eyes, to see what is whirling out of the timeless, what is already here, what has departed.

We wait at the threshold of the other world, when the other world is already present. Who is laughing at us? Amused with our seeking in all directions, with our thinking God is other. We struggle with our self, thinking of the journey and the preparations we need. But for our Beloved we are always unprepared. Our wisdom is our own undoing. Our preoccupations prepare us for what we already know, and thus are useless.

This state is saturated with non-existence.

October '97

Incestuous Darkness

Out of the unknown, out of the silence of sleep or the stillness of meditation, we awaken. Awakening we claim our self, come back into our self. We awake into a body that we know as ours, a mind that is familiar, thoughts with which we can identify and that give us our identity. And so, even after a journey to the beyond we stay in the circle of our own self. But what if when we awaken we do not find the familiar anxieties, hopes, patterns that make us? What if we find only emptiness?

As a wayfarer we have been lost before, the lover vanished in love, the mystic merged into emptiness. But this was moments in meditation, moments in and out of time, moments surrounded by our self. We came back, always we came back, knowing that we were taken, dissolved; but when we came back the familiar was present again; the landscape of our self was there, greeting us, enveloping us.

But one day, maybe not today or tomorrow, something happens, something so fundamental and so simple, and completely bewildering. We come to realize that there is no self to return to. The meditation was not just a glimpse; what was taken was not returned. Life is still present, full of its discords and hidden beauty, but something is missing. And suddenly, unexpectedly, there is the realization that it was always like this. Because when this veil is lifted what is seen is not new, but unbearably ancient. What is experienced is a primal vacancy, an emptiness that is beyond light and dark. And the mystic knows with a knowledge that is inborn, not discovered, that there is no going back. When we discover something so fundamental we cannot forget again, we cannot pull the veil across and pretend not to know.

Each of us carries the seeds of our own destruction. For the many this destruction is played out in the game of life, leading to the darkness and revelation of death. For those attracted by the light of their own Self this destruction is what leads them away from the illusions of the world, the *maya* of attachments, into the depths of themselves and the pain of purification. If these seekers persist they will find the hidden core of their being and learn to live in the light that guides them, the light of spiritual service and devotion.

But for some this is not enough, this was never enough. They have a darker secret, which does not acknowledge limitation. From the very beginning they belong to Another, to He whose Name cannot be named. And this belonging is their light and their darkness, their blessing and their curse. They are the guardians of light and darkness because they have no destiny; such is the finality of their belonging. Their destruction *must be total* because He is All. So simple, so horrific, and ultimate. These are the friends of God, the lost of the lost. Some are veiled and some are almost visible. They are allowed to call others to the brink of non-being when they have passed over.

What does it mean to be lost? It means to belong to such a degree that nothing is left. The price is abandonment, the habitation desolation. And one day the lover awakens to the knowledge that it was always like this, and sees how much he avoided it, how many times he looked for relief. But how can a bird avoid the wind? For how long can a fire burn cold?

There is a silence so potent that nothing can speak, which calls from the hungry emptiness and welcomes a friend. Death is only a word; loss of ego is a phrase that is blown away. The primal power of non-being is so terrible and blissful that nothing can survive unless God wills. And it was always like this, shall always be like this, cannot be otherwise.

January '98

More Thoughts

Stepping into the wonderland of the heart, what do I find? Why do I feel so lost, so unable to walk between the worlds? Each time I look for an answer all that surround me are the endless horizons of non-being, which stretch out to the infinite. Looking again, I find a path. But where does it lead? Where does it take me? It is easy to search for the last frontier, but to give oneself to the heart, to the dance of light and dark, wanting neither the light nor the dark—that is something else. How is one supposed to walk between the worlds, to hold true to what is of neither this world nor the next? Looking inward, what do I find? Who is there to find what is hidden? Silence stretches around me, and I walk with hesitation. Patterns constellate, but who is there to dissolve these patterns? When can we just relate in the ways of love?

But in the end, *who* wants to relate in the ways of love, in those strange pathways, in those empty spaces where even travelers do not venture? There is silence, there is nothing for the senses, and there are no answers. To make the mistake of wanting something is to constellate effects, to step out of the silence. And yet wanting is also our humanity, even if it must be offered up. We are who we are; where we place our feet determines what unfolds in the passage of time, and so the cries of the heart run past us. Why have I chosen this passage? I have been forced, asked, accepted, to have a foot in both worlds, and also to stand alone, seeing only the patterns made by the psyche and the mind, without the meaning given by these experiences—without looking either to the past or future, just being here in the locus of events. Why does so much have to happen? Energy flows through the currents of non-being without hesitation. Why, when one knows this inner peace and tranquility, cannot the days pass in peace and tranquility? Is it because then I would not be engaged, would not enter into the circle of life? But I am tired, not knowing where to look.

I wish I could say that there is an answer. But there is nothing to be said. How can one point out the passage from confusion and ego to the vast light and simplicity of Self? In the world of desires and the ego, light is reflected into a million shapes and colors, while here there is only the purity and brilliance of emptiness. Why can I not just embrace the two worlds, with all of the contradictions that color our existence? Or just forget the way the patterns of light and darkness fall across the wall, the drama of events that some call life? I feel that my world is being torn apart, and I do not know what to do. Who is tearing whom? In the oneness all must be a part of the same. It is not someone else's experience, but a vortex of undoing into which I am drawn or thrown. Why not just let it happen? Is it because I crave the inner world where there is no conflict? Or the simplicity of an outer life? But I have neither.

There are times in my life when I have been pushed over the edge, and this is such a time. I can look at it rationally, even understand it, but it horrifies me. I am shocked by the intensity of what can be lost. But what can be lost when one is nothing? What is my life? I have no life. It is not me who speaks, so what am I holding onto? I do not understand. I feel that I do not have any ground to stand upon. Whose ground is it? And who would walk this ground in their right mind, when the swirling forces of existence color everything, and non-existence is held in the background?

Of what am I so frightened? Of losing everything, but is it mine to lose? Of being made a fool? But whose fool? Why Beloved have you put me through this? And where do I hold back, as if waiting for salvation? But who is there to save? Somewhere I just want to die and escape this crazy situation, or retire to the simplicity of what is and what is not. But who is there to retire? Of what am I so afraid? Where I am looking there is no one. No one is in this clear light, this emptiness before existence. Maybe I am deluded, mad, unaware of anything except dreams. But I have always lived like this, trusting only God's will, the way my Beloved has made me. I only have the thin thread of my devotion, but what is that in the whirlwind of emotions, in the games that are played? And why am I so afraid? Because even those around me do not know it, do not see the space where the light is clear. And if they do not, to whom am I talking? Always to be misunderstood creates this deep pain and anxiety. This is the crucifixion. This is what pains me. How can I live in a world of so many delusions? But who is there to choose? When so much light is seen and so much darkness is visible....

January '98

The dark night, the fear of waves,
the terrifying whirlpool,
How can they know of our state,
those who go lightly along the shore?

Hāfiz

Confusion

Spiritual life is a living, dynamic process. The wayfarer becomes caught in it, absorbed by it, changed by it beyond recognition. And there is no end to this dynamic evolution within our self. States change, the stages turn our heart, and gradually, very gradually, our consciousness is altered, our perception shifts. How this happens is a mystery, just as the whole process of inner transformation is a mystery. But the wayfarer has to learn to live with these changes, to adapt, to leave behind the old understanding and allow what is new to become known.

Once again I have slowly come to realize that it is not how I thought, that the journey Home has another dimension, a deeper direction. I have had to face the illusion of my own journey, how I was caught in certain convictions, especially spiritual convictions. Now I sense something else, something so very different. I can call it the "incestuous darkness" but this is only a name, an attempt to fix in words a swirling quality that carries confusion, chaos, and tremendous freedom.

Always the journey, the path changes. Always we are thrown into something beyond what we might have expected. My teacher gave many lectures about different aspects of the path and spiritual life. They were inspiring and informative lectures, but towards the end of her life she said. "That was how I saw it then. Now I see it very differently. Now there is only merging."

For years I have tried to understand, define, explain to myself and to others, to present a context for spiritual life, for a mystical journey that leads to the beyond. With the clear light of consciousness and the careful choice of words I tried to outline a path, a path that belongs to the tradition of lovers, that carries the teachings of our elders, of those who have walked before us. I felt the need to put their words into today's language, to make this path more accessible to people. Now I sense something else, something that was always at the borders of consciousness, hinted at, and yet avoided in its intensity. Now I am thrown into it, can no longer avoid this intensity. A quality of chaos envelops me from within, not the chaos of madness but the chaos of becoming, the chaos of life and what is beyond life.

Where does the path go, what strange byways does it follow? Always we look for a sense of direction. Are we going Home? Is this the right path? Are we in tune? But the path is much deeper and more ancient than any sense of direction. It belongs to the timeless inner dimension, to the unforgiving emptiness in which everything is forgiven. Yes, there is choice, yes we can lose the path, we can follow the ego with all its subtleties of self-defense. We can walk away from our heart's call, from the edge of the abyss, even with the best of intentions. We can say, "Not yet," "Another time," "Just wait awhile, and I will catch up. I really want the Truth; I really want to go Home. But just now, right at this minute, there are other things I have to attend to, more pressing business." And so the path dissolves, its urgency hidden, its demands neglected. But what is lost? How can the path ever be lost? How can the swirl of the sea and the call of the sea birds be forgotten? Can we really block out the endless abyss?

The path is a strange creature, full of the unexpected, born from the unexpected, attempting to take us into the unknown, into the unknowable. And always we want the security of knowing, and so our fear of the dark betrays us, fools us, gives us more tangible problems, more accessible answers.

What is this path, this empty way, this call from afar? "I have phrases and whole pages memorized, but nothing can be told about love." When we enter the presence of our Beloved all words are forgotten. There is heartache, a call, and a sigh that comes from the depth. These are the signs, but where do they lead? Why do we expect something tangible, even goodness or purity? Why do we look for reassurance when we stand at this water's edge? There is no way forward, only the disappointment of what we have not found, what our seeking has not revealed. Expectations are such a heavy load to carry, excess baggage that obscures the view.

Follow your heart's call; follow the path—but where? What do these words of encouragement mean, when deep within we sense the terror of an endless night and will make sure that our path skirts around this desolate place? We may hear the phrase "to die before you die," but what do we know of this ultimate desolation, the betrayal of our own self? Oh, the path will take us to the water's edge, and may even provide us with the illusion of a boat, with the fantasy of a further shore, but really these are just mind games and psychological gimmicks. There is no spiritual board game, no path to enlightenment, because our Beloved who comes "like a thief in the night" ravishes us so unexpectedly, never in any way we could have envisioned.

Why do we look for answers? Why do we try to dress with the right clothes for the journey, the correct spiritual attitude, when we need to be unprotected? So many stories have been told, books written, pictures painted, and always we skirt around the edge, frightened of facing the depth of our failure and longing, the tragedy of our very nature, this strange call that alone can destroy us. Always we try to convince our self that the path is really about something else, about finding something, about becoming something, always avoiding the ultimate price, the real nature of the journey.

Sorrow, endless sorrow is what we are given to work with, to open us, to take us, to silence us. This endless sorrow has oceans of joy hidden within it, the joy that is life itself, the hidden face of creation. This joy is not a flimsy alternative to life, not life skating on the surface, but the intensity of emptiness pouring into form, of love coming into being, of the Beloved manifesting Himself. And the sorrow is His promise that we would not forget Him, the heart's memory, the soul's imprint. This sorrow is desire and longing, the call and the echo, the forgetfulness and the memory. This sorrow is the abyss if we dare to live it, the unending emptiness of God's love for us.

But who can bear this real sorrow, this wine that tastes like blood? Only the foolhardy, the naïve, and the desperate. Only the soldiers of the heart's fortune and the shameless women of love's bazaar. In this marketplace we are bought and sold, our most precious possessions scattered and deemed worthless. We are taken by love to love, drunken and desolate, intoxicated and helpless. Addicted to longing, hungry for what is Real, we know neither our self nor the chaos that awaits us. We like to think we are spiritual seekers, lovers, wayfarers, but when we give our self away without conditions there is no name, for what is there to name? The lost have no name.

Those who remain behind carry names; they carry the banners of their own inner development, their spiritual or worldly success. They know who they are, and are resplendent in their own recognition. The lost are not like this; all they have known is an emptiness and a hunger, the swirling waters that can carry them away. They know they are to be taken, and the rest is not their business. Maybe they have had experiences, glimpses of the beyond. But the real journey is beyond any such knowing, is too simple to be explained, too ordinary to be noticed, and far too intense to be talked about. There are things that can never be said, perhaps because they are too intimate, too painful, too bewildering, or just unspeakable; maybe the love was more than we believed possible, than we knew was allowed. Such love is not for the fainthearted, not for those who believe in duality and the barriers of separation. Such love is only for the lost, for those who have given themselves away, who have said yes to God's will. And always we wait to be taken ...

February '98

A Cry of Despair

Of what am I so afraid, that makes me turn inside, try to hide, to lose myself? There is only His love and the devotion of His servant. And yet I feel so lost, so alone, so forsaken. I am just a lover, just one who gives himself for love, and yet now, it is as if the tables have turned. Inwardly the night has come and there is only darkness, not even the first star of morning. Where have you taken me, my Beloved? Into what place have you plunged me? I only want to be your servant, and yet I feel that I am so forsaken, so forgotten, so misunderstood. There is an aloneness that is neither of yesterday nor of tomorrow. It holds me, as if with an ancient fear.

Is this the same fear I felt when I saw the work that was in front of me, oh, ten years ago? Is this the fear of the work, of the aloneness of the work? There are friends who follow the same path, but I must be alone; otherwise the work will lose its edge, its crazy, desperate edge. I am one of the lost. There is nothing else to say. But why this fear that grips me from the inside? The work goes on, like the point of a needle or an arrow. I am alone in it and yet not alone. Lost and yet how can I be lost when I am with God? Forget and remember …

I have been thrown into a new space, and I look around, wondering why I hoped that I would stay in comfortable surroundings for long. It was a joke! There is only the endless horizon of love, only the darkness, the despair, and the freezing rain that falls. How does one know that love is about darkness? Because it is stamped inside, imprinted into the soul, this ancient secret of love. And for us there is only the despair of belonging to no one.

There is this fear. Outside it is a beautiful day, with the sky blue and the birds. But none of it touches me, only an ancient sorrow. It is so easy to sit in silence, or to be with friends, and yet I am pushed into a space as cold as ice and as desolate as dawn. Here there is the imprint of tomorrow, and a cry that cannot be heard. And I am so alone, so terribly alone. Why? Why? Why?

Why am I lost? There is nowhere to go. There is nothing to do, and I am lost, lost in desolation so terrible and ancient. A cry from the heart, an anguish of the soul, an emptiness beyond imagining.

June '99

Thoughts from the Edge

There is a forgotten substance that lies at the edge of the universe. It is neither here nor there. It is absence without presence. It is lost without being found. It lives in unbelief, in the dim recesses of spiritual memory. How do we know it is there? Because it is not. Anything that is not leaves a stamp, a trace, although very different from the trace left by something that exists. But there are times when the universe unfolds that this substance is needed. It is vital because it exists without existing. Because it does not exist it does not have the effect of that which exists. It is not caught in the limitations of being. It does not interact, or affect the gravitational pull of any object or idea. And yet it has substance, not physical substance, or mental substance, but a substance that is born between the worlds.

There are very few people who can work with this substance, because one has to be aware of one's non-existence while fully participating in life. One has to stand at the brink of existence, where even love filters out. In this place one mirrors this substance into being, so that its reflection interacts with existence. It is a very subtle work, requiring concentration, and yet there is nothing upon which to concentrate.

How do we know what to do? We don't. This is essential to the process. It is a creative work of not-knowing, of standing alone in emptiness, with the wind of un-creation howling. But very subtly this substance is filtered into creation. It does not leave any traces because it does not exist. But it has a particular effect, like a door to a summer garden that is left open. The open door does not exist, but the fragrance of summer roses does exist.

The mirror is our own being. It is the essence of our own being, the place where being and non-being come together. It is presence, and yet a presence that does not impose itself, that just *is*. There is no interaction. This is very important. To exist without interaction, without ask-ing for anything, or denying anything. And this presence has no permanence, nor does it leave any traces. It slips so easily into non-being.

But there is much laughter. Not laughter at anything. But laughter that *is*. This is the laughter of life. Like the doorway to the summer garden this laughter is an open-ing, and in this opening we forget something. It is very important, this forgetting. Most people cannot forget, they always allow their memories to remain. But a mind trained in emptiness can forget, can allow important things to cease to exist. This is where the laughter comes in. This laughter does not understand the past, or the world of cause and effect.

April '01

Memories of a Moment

Why do we look for what we cannot find? Why do people make this strange journey from nowhere to nowhere? In emptiness there is Reality. All else is passing shadows, sunlight reflected for an instant. And yet this is the human drama: to chase the shadows, be entranced by a moment of sunshine. Light and laughter, joy and hope. And the human being, you or me, searching for what we cannot find, knowing the journey, the embrace, the stillness at the center, and then losing it again and again.

It is not that we are lost, because that would imply there is another way to be, that there is a still center of being that is not thrown this way and that. But the tide always rises and falls; along the shoreline the birds follow the ebb and flow, seeking for insects in the sand. Everything passes, nothing remains, and yet in our deepest being we are that nothing, that emptiness that is Real.

Every day we watch the light come, and the evening come, and the night arrive, and then our dreams, if we remember them. This is the cycle of our days, our lives, and yet there are moments when the curtain rises, and suddenly, out of nowhere, we *know*. In this moment we are truly alive. Such is the fleeting joy of existence that lasts forever, that is always present, that is the real drama.

Look this way and that and you will find something. It will find you. It is the promise of life, of a life waiting to be lived.

Remember that in the silence you and I exist. This is not a promise but a statement of fact, a thread that connects together so many existences. And it is fully alive. It is a connection between one world and another, one lifetime and another, one soul and another.

So many memories, so many lifetimes, each with its own flavor, its own scent. Each a stamp of the Real upon the shoreline of this world.

December '03

Beyond the Horizons

Beyond the horizons of this world is a place that few know, a place without borders, without loss or gain, where even the cry of the seagull is forgotten. When you come here, or are taken here, remember this: here are no memories, not even silence, for silence would suggest the existence of sound. And yet something within you mysteriously recognizes what you have lost, recognizes the primal emptiness, the vast unknowing, the wonder of what is not. What is there to say of this place beyond the worlds? Here there are no dreams, there is no substance to form even images. And yet there is a belonging that is stamped in the core of one's being, a belonging that nothing can break.

Far away there is a place called existence. It is full of dreams, of opportunities, of life and death. Here are no such dramas; here the heart is empty. If I could bring you here you could understand, how when everything is removed, when all is dissolved, lost, undone, we are what we are.

But then the laughter of children and the tears of old men call us back into what people call life, into this strange substance that weaves itself into forms. Yet even when we seem stranded on this shore of existence, when the darkness is lost, we can never forget. That place beyond the worlds is always with you, it is at the end and beginning of every breath, within everything you know, more primal than even silence. It is the scar of a wound from a lover you never knew.

November '06

From the Depths of Non-being

From the depths of non-being a voice arose, "It is neither this nor that. It is as it was." And in this unending emptiness, in the silence that comes before sound, where there are no footsteps, where there is no murmuring stream, there is a presence. And that presence needs to be heard. It needs to be accepted, and not made barren. It needs to be recognized, and in the silence welcomed. And yet it is neither before nor after, and even the present moment is not a place for it to be. How can that be? Because there is no moment—moments belong to existence, to the wonder of what is. And this presence has no existence, nor is it the opposite of existence. It truly has no name.

And yet within this presence something is beginning, something is being welcomed, something is being made known. That is the wonder, the mystery, the magic. As if non-being now had a home, a place, an in- and out-breath. So why are we waiting when it is already here, this ancient return, this moment that is no moment? Is it because it is so simple to be unexpected? So ordinary that no one sees? Or is it because there is no real knowing of why it is here?

Without this knowing, we are left with the unanswered question, of how non-existence and existence relate together. We know how two things can relate, but a thing and a no-thing? A space is speaking to us in ways that have been forgotten; it carries a knowing of what is before and after existence.

But this is not what I have been trying to say, not what I have been giving myself to. I have been seeking the mystery of the created and the uncreated. And even this is not true, not what I have been shown. Something within is tentatively coming into existence, as if a memory is being uncovered, a recognition of what was before, before anything. And I am that presence, and the voice and the knowing, and the silence, and the coming together. And yet I am still waiting. After so long is it really allowed? Is there really no need to hide myself and pretend, to walk with practiced feet the paths of existence—when I know something else—which knows me?

February '08

Waiting

Between the worlds there is a power waiting to come into our world. It is a power that belongs to the Almighty, to the energy behind creation. But it does not follow the laws of this world. It has a sense of humor that will trick humanity, taking away its power games with a flick of the wrist. There is a laughter and a joy in His power coming into His world, revealing Him in a new way, opening us to the mystery and potency of His presence.

Even our rejection of God, our forgetfulness and hubris, are cause for love and laughter, for the reawakening of divine joy, as once again God reminds us of the divine. Just remember that it is His way and not our way. Not the limited projection and image we have of our Creator or God, but something other and wonderful, something that is alive with glory and love.

And our work is to wait for Him, not as penitent sinners but as lovers, as servants, as ones who for so long have been alone, without our Beloved or master. Remember that this is not our world but God's. His world and His unfolding.

Our forgetfulness has had a price. We look around at our world and see the ecological disaster, the unnecessary suffering, the lack of compassion, the different signs of our forgetfulness. And within the heart we wonder: can it have been otherwise? But there is a deeper truth that is being made visible. Once again God is revealing Himself to Himself. Once again our Beloved is taking on the clothes of creation to be present in His world. And this is such grace, such wonder, that nothing else matters.

Spring '09

Aloneness

As we walk towards the dawn what are we carrying? What are our attachments, real or imagined? There is a love that cannot be put into words, and a fear of failure that is real, that has haunted me since the path began. There is a deep sense of destiny, but does that destiny belong to me or to God? I would like to step outside of this haunted circle and return to the simplicity of what is, but that is also a dream, a memory of something that never was. Always there has been a sense of purpose pressing upon me, even as I try to avoid it, to find ways to leave this destiny behind, or to give it to others so that I can remain unencumbered, watching the seasons pass like flowers and the leaves fall and then flow downstream. But I have come to realize that there is no innocence to return to, no enchanted garden or quiet mountain hut. There is always the demand of the worlds coming together, of the place where the two seas meet, and the currents of love and creation that belong to that meeting.

So why did I not just say "yes" to this meeting, embrace this destiny and want nothing else? Why did I try to seek solace in something else? Why did I almost try to destroy myself rather than fully accepting what was given? The ego has so many guises, so many ways to deceive us. And even creation itself would deceive us rather than allow us to live its greatest secret, the essence of its belonging to God.

Is that why I ran away and tried to hide? Is that why I hid myself in a mockery of what I knew to be true? Or was there another reason? Did I need to play this game of creation, this hide and seek of love? Did I need to be lost and found and lost again, have my heart broken in a thousand ways? Did I need to taste the salt of existence, the way we delude our self even when we think that we are true? And does it matter? Are these words just something else to hide behind? The simple truth is that it does not belong to me—that this destiny was always His, just as every stone, every fragrance, every meaning or lack of meaning is His. And so I return to a deeper knowing and there is peace, for a moment there is peace.

And yet there is an answer to an unasked question that is not yet fully born, like the dawn that is breaking before it appears. And this question is very simple. Why all the struggle and the tears and the exhaustion and despair, when everything belongs to God? Why, if I belong to God and that is all that matters, is it so hard to live this destiny, this calling? Is it the surrender that is lacking, the surrender that must be given again and again, even if one has said "yes" in the very core of one's being? Is it some human limitation that must be lived, like a wolf howling in the night? Or is it simply that this is the way things are, that nothing can be born without pain, and the birth of the soul is a terrible business?

I know that somewhere there is laughter and limitless love. And I have also come to know in ways that surprise me the limitations that surround us, even the limitations of love in this world. This is what has hurt me more than anything, what has cut scars into me again and again. This is what I could not believe until my Beloved forced me to accept it. Our every breath is love captured into form, and in that form there is limitation. In God's overwhelming oneness there is a separation, or the illusion of separation, that we each must live. We each must be true to our own uniqueness, a uniqueness that makes us separate even as it is stamped with a presence that belongs to God. This for me is the greatest paradox: that the consciousness of divine oneness includes a consciousness of separation, that we are different from each other and separate from God. In this world we carry the stamp of God's uniqueness, and that means separation.

We each carry a single ray of divine love that is distinct from all others, that is our destiny and our journey. To fully incarnate and live this love only happens in our aloneness, even as we know that we are one. This is what I found so difficult to accept, as if I were too attached to the limitless nature of divine love, to the formless world before creation. And I have to accept the world of limitation, the world that is born where the two seas meet. And in this truth there is a simplicity, even if it is not the simplicity I thought I wanted.

I always wanted to return to the oneness that embraces everything, in which everything is saturated with love. And instead I found a oneness that lives in my aloneness, that is present in its own axis of truth. And I have had to give up a certain dream, because there is always a price to pay in this world of ours, there is always a burden to be left at the barrier. Before the dawn there is always a cloud that covers the sun, a darkness that is present. And sometimes this cloud is created from our own deepest desires, from our own longings, which also have to be left behind. The sunlight is bleak in its ordinariness.

So I return to what I have always known, to the solitariness I thought to leave behind. I return to the deep knowing that I am with God in my aloneness in the inner and outer worlds. If that is the price to pay, maybe I have paid it.

August '09

Autumn Thoughts

How can one describe an invisible presence? How can one put words to a sweetness within the heart, a silence that is neither looked for nor found? And yet something within me calls me to write about my Beloved, to say how my Beloved's presence is felt. I could speak for hours about how demanding He is, how He has taken away every excuse not to be with Him, about the intensity of His commands, or how intense they are to me. And yet I begin to think that this is all a creation of my own. God just is—and even the piercing of divine love is just a sign of my resistance. Even the desolation of abandonment is just something I have created, because how can my Beloved not be always with me?

Do these words mean anything? Is meaning to be found in words? After a lifetime of looking, searching, struggling, what has been revealed except the emptiness in the center of the circle and a deep knowing that every-thing belongs to God? But in these words something is missing that is so fundamental it shames me to write them, and it tears my heart apart to be in this world without my Beloved, even though I know that all is He.

So what is the cause of my distress, and who am I to be distressed? I know that God's love is everywhere, in every breath even when I forget to repeat His name. I know that the cry from the heart is my Beloved's cry, even when it feels that my heart is bursting. And all of this knowing means nothing, because something is missing, some note is not being played. And without this note my whole life feels like a leaf at autumn, discarded, to be blown and then swept away, or left on the forest floor, knowing nothing of its fate or the fate of the tree from which it has come.

From one tree came so many lives, so many experiences of the same One Thing, and each leaf is different and each leaf comes from the same tree. And the tree is just one tree in the infinite forest of divine love made manifest.

A life of longing, searching, struggling, and now no energy is left for the struggle or the search. And yet there is this infinite sadness of knowing something is unlived, an aspect of my Beloved's presence has not been made manifest. But whose life is it? The "I" wants to claim something for itself, to say, "I exist." But even this illusion, this joke of an "I" that knows its limitations only too well, that longs for peace in the midst of life's demands, stands waiting. Does this waiting belong to God or me, and does it matter?

And so my heart longs to express something, to say "It is like this," but what can it say, what can be put into words, as cars pass in the street outside and the summer rain falls gently? It is like a question coming out of non-existence, wanting to be known, and then vanishing into the emptiness again, as it knows there is no answer.

September '09

Still Struggling with Words

Whose are the words that belong only to silence? What is the way that leads nowhere? In the evening the fire is burning low, but there is no need to put any more wood on the flames. Soon there will be only embers and then night will come. We are always looking for answers, but it is the questions that are the real obstacle, mirages in the desert of the mind. When the moon is full its light shines more brightly than when it is new. If only I could forget everything, bring no memories to my mind. Sometimes it is like that, but then from deep within there are feelings that come, a sudden sadness, or laughter. Children playing in the snow, making snowmen or throwing snowballs. And soon it will all melt, but the laughter will be present, like a bell that has already rung. And the tears... what will it take for them to be lost?

So many things I have tried to understand, but in the end all falls away. Yet at the same time this life is full of these threads woven together. Maybe that is what it means to live from day to day, to accept this mirage of so many voices, this tapestry struggling to create itself. So many threads, even though the heart knows it is only one thread, one mystery being born again and again, the single brush stroke of a Great Master. So what is it that we really see or feel? Images in a landscape that might exist.

Maybe it is simpler just to taste the hot tea, warming my hands on the cup.

October '09

Love

And so the journey continues.... Your heart takes you to places that do not exist, where the snow falls gently and the wind comes from behind the clouds. And here, in this land, you can forget everything, even your own existence. There is no mirror to reflect you, no open door to walk through, just an endless landscape of love that knows no boundaries. And the wind is real and the snow continues to fall and the love continues, and will always continue. So you can leave behind those old worn clothes that you called your existence, those ways you used to walk when you thought you were alive. Because here in this place that is like no other there is the freedom you always knew, a freedom that belongs to love.

Do not be discouraged, do not ever be discouraged, even when you feel so lost and misunderstood, when the wheels of existence carry you always along roads you would rather not travel. There is this other land, this landscape that belongs to love. This is the place where the two seas meet, where existence reveals its secrets, where time uncovers what always was, even if you have never seen it before.

So why do we wait, feeling stranded, expecting something, when we are already at the place where the two seas meet, where the journey we call our self has already ended?

Do not worry. There is nothing to find or lose—the moon will always rise, the wind will blow apart the clouds and time will take you where you need to go. You are the place where the two seas meet, where love is uncovered, where silence is mirrored into sound. And yet we are conditioned to worry, to dream in a language that causes misunderstandings, to seek meanings where there is only the moon reflected in the water. We mistake our self again and again, looking for what cannot be answered. And yet there is always this other place, this vastness that calls to us, that draws us out of our existence. Remember it is always here. It cannot be anywhere else, just as love can never be somewhere else, because that would deny the very nature of love.

November '09

4

What Does It Mean to Be a Teacher?

The previous passages describe the intensity of some of my own inner experiences. And yet many of my most demanding and often conflicting experiences have come from my work as a spiritual teacher. If part of the very dynamic of mystical life is to confuse and bewilder, as much as it liberates and intoxicates, then the teacher is the one who stands in the center of this vortex of divine love.

The love between teacher and disciple is both the most powerful and the most paradoxical relationship a human being can experience; it is unique in this world, in that it belongs only to God. And yet it has to be played out in the human arena where it is inevitably brought into the limited and distorted structures of the ego and personality. From the point of view of the soul all the projection and misunderstanding this gives rise to can seem such a needless drama, based entirely on illusion, and yet this drama too has a role to play. It is the teacher's job through it all to remain unswervingly true to the real divine nature, to the love and to the inner light of the disciple, as the transmission of love that the disciple needs to make the journey is given from heart to heart.

In an earlier chapter, "Dust at His Feet," I wrote about my relationship with my sheikh, the Naqshbandi Sufi master Radha Mohan Lal. The following chapter describes a little of my own experience as a Sufi teacher. I began this work when I was thirty-six and was sent by my teacher, Irina Tweedie, to lecture about the Sufi path in North America. And then when she retired in 1992, I became her successor.[38] In 1998, the year before she died, I was made a Sufi sheikh.

I should clarify that there are two distinct forms of spiritual teacher. There are teachers who convey the spiritual teachings of their tradition, their practices and disciplines. They may give lectures and seminars, write books and have students who study these teachings and often engage in the practices. Then there are spiritual teachers who have disciples, taking upon themselves the full responsibility of their disciples' spiritual evolution, their journey Home. I have written a number of books and conveyed some of the teachings of my lineage of Sufism; this chapter is about my work in the traditional relationship of teacher and disciple. Although most of this drama of soul to soul happens deep within the heart, beyond the grasp of consciousness, I hope to convey a little of the human side of this most extraordinary relationship. In particular I want to describe an ambiguity that I often feel about what belongs to the human being and what belongs to God, and how this has been played out in my life.

The teacher is without a face and without a name.

WHAT DOES IT MEAN to be a teacher, a guide, to have the spiritual responsibility of taking souls Home? For many years I knew what it meant to be a disciple, to have my heart opened by love, to sit at the feet of my teacher being absorbed into emptiness, to see the light of another world in her eyes. From the first moment I met the white-haired Russian lady who was to be my teacher, I felt in her the inner authority that belongs to a Sufi teacher, and in the coming years, full of fear and longing I sat, week after week, in her small room, wanting nothing except the Truth I knew she knew. As she spoke about her sheikh in India, I felt his invisible presence, a being of power and love to whom I came to realize I belonged beyond life and death. I recognized this energy of the path that would demand everything from me, and over the years I experienced how a disciple is destroyed and remade through love, bitter and sweet.

Then, one day when I was thirty-four, I was told by Irina Tweedie that I too would become a teacher, take up this transmission of love. This simple statement, made almost in passing, terrified me. Yet it also made sense of and echoed some dreams I had had in previous years. I recognized how the training had begun years before, maybe soon after I first came to the path as a battered and unbalanced young man. I could glimpse how I had been guided by the masters of the path and though I knew it was a grace to be given this work, it was also the last thing I wanted. It was as if I already knew it would demand from me more than I believed I could give, destroy me in ways I did not yet know—the fear was very real.[39]

I had sat at my teacher's feet since I was nineteen, and knew her ways of working with people, and also saw the demands that the path made on her. Because seekers sensed the unlimited love within her, they somehow instinctively felt that their demands could also be unlimited. I saw her give and give until her body and whole being were exhausted, and still she gave. Once people sense real love, their unmet needs come to the surface and almost suffocate everything else. People came with all of their troubles as well as their longing, and it was all unloaded on her. So much was expected. And this was the work and the world that were waiting for me.

Although, after sitting in her presence, watching her work with people day after day, I had some sense of what was involved, of course my own experience of this work was quite different. She began when she was already over sixty, having just returned from India after the death of our sheikh, and for the first ten years just a few people gathered around her, sitting in her small North London room. I began when I was young and the path was already present in the West: there was already a room full of people. My journey was different and yet the essence of the work was the same: holding a transmission of love to be given to those who need.

Maybe I should say from the beginning that from my experience I think it is almost impossible to be a spiritual teacher in the West. Recently a young man came to me who had begun having a small group of people around him, and asked my advice about being a spiritual teacher. Half-jokingly I replied, "I think it's impossible. Here in the West there is no container, no tradition of the real relationship of teacher and disciple. We have no context for this relationship of the soul that is both impersonal and intimate. There's just misunderstanding and projections. It's much better to have a sensible job as a plumber or an accountant." I don't think he understood what I meant.

In the West we have just an echo of an echo of this ancient tradition, in the love that Mary Magdalene had for Christ and the few words that she spoke to him after she mistook him for a gardener near his empty grave:

> Jesus saith unto her, Mary. She turned herself,
> and saith unto him, Raboni; which is to say,
> Master.[40]

Here are the devotion and love that belong to this traditional relationship of teacher and disciple, but it was buried by the Church and has been forgotten. And yet anyone who has been awakened by a teacher's love knows its truth. But how to express and live this sacred relationship in a culture that understands only personal love? How not to get caught in the myriad projections and misunderstandings that can arise when there is so much love and nearness? How can we live this mystery in its purity, so that, as with Mary, it can take us to see the risen Christ?

The question for the teacher is how to hold this truth, this essential love, when you know it will be misunderstood by even the most sincere seeker. And from this simple question comes my own experience that the teacher can expect to be burned by this love even more than the disciple. The teacher has to hold this love in its true, impersonal nature, knowing that it belongs only to God. And together with the love comes a deep recognition and complete acceptance of the wayfarer—one can only walk the path as one's whole self. But this same love and acceptance so often awakens in the disciple a desire to have a personal relationship with the teacher, as the disciple does not understand that the real relationship belongs to the soul and not to the personality. The need to personalize this relationship appears most strongly in women, particularly when the love and understanding they experience are otherwise lacking in their lives. And in the West women seem to form a majority of spiritual seekers, especially on a path of devotion like Sufism.

Yet there can be no "friendship" with the teacher, despite the feelings of inner closeness that are very real. In the Sufi tradition the relationship with the teacher leads the disciple towards a relationship with God.[41] The teacher is in essence an empty space through which the energy of the Divine can nourish the disciple, or a mirror that just reflects back her true self. Having no conscious understanding of its real nature, the disciple will color this relationship with personal dramas, with the images of parents or other authority figures, or even with the longing for a physical lover. She will paint her own pictures on this clear mirror.

I remember at the beginning of the work being shocked at how easily this inner relationship of love and closeness was misplaced, how this intimacy of the soul evoked so many other feelings and projections. Because I never knew my sheikh on a human level, I had never played out this drama, and found it deeply disturbing. For a time I tried to be distant, even cold or disdainful, sometimes deliberately pushing away the feelings that were projected. But then I learned how easily this could evoke patterns of rejection in the disciple, which could then open old wounds and veil the disciple from the love that was given, the love that could take them Home. I have found that it is better to allow the misunderstandings and projections, which over time are resolved through the energy of the path, through the impersonal nature of the love that is given.

And now, after so many years, when someone tells me that they want a "more personal relationship" with me, there is just a certain sadness that this evokes. If they knew the real nature of the love that is given, how its purpose is to draw them step by step towards an abandonment so complete that only Truth remains, they would not try to color it with the images of a personal friendship. And if they could glimpse what is within "me," an emptiness where a cold wind often blows that knows nothing of any personal self, they would not want to get any closer. But we always paint the pictures we want to see, and when love is given there is no understanding of its desolation.

Hopefully the teacher is one who has been trained to want nothing, has been emptied so completely that there is no danger of being caught in the trap of so many projections. I was fortunate in that I was trained for almost twenty years before I began. I was ground to dust in order to do this work. And for the first few years I was watched very closely, and then crushed again. I was taught the old-fashioned way, forced to see my limitations again and again. And this was only the beginning.

To guide a soul back to God is the most serious responsibility anyone can be given, because it concerns what is most precious within a human being: the desire for Truth and the ability to live this desire—the potential to go Home. Nothing is more important in the life of an individual, and so nothing is more dangerous to abuse. Sometimes seekers have come to me who have been spiritually misled, or even abused, by their teacher. The soul becomes twisted, unable to live or reflect the light that is within. These seekers can easily become lost souls, wandering aimlessly without true purpose. Sometimes help can be given, and their light can be returned to them. They can be reconnected with their life's meaning. But there is almost always a scar, a sadness that what was so precious was contaminated.

On the Sufi path the disciple is taken Home through the power of divine love, and this love is the most potent and dangerous force in existence. It can cut through every pattern of resistance and awaken the heart. To have the power to place this love into the heart of another person is a tremendous responsibility. It also means that the other person can easily fall in love with you. This love is like nothing the disciple has ever known, and it is given freely without conditions. It is pure poison—a drug to the heart. The teacher holds the heart of the disciple in his own heart and nourishes it with divine love. And how easy it is to mistake this divine love for human love. Without any cultural understanding of devotion, the disciple can become lost in a maze of longings in which the human and Divine become confused. It is the work of the teacher to try again and again to reflect back to the disciple the true impersonal nature of this love.

After almost twenty years I am in constant awe of this inner drama of divine love, how the disciple is held in love, and how the soul of the teacher is guided by the laws of love in this work. But it was many years before I understood the nature and effect of this transmission of love: how the essence of the relationship between teacher and disciple belongs to the level of the soul, how the soul of the disciple is infused with the light and love that it needs for the journey. And how little this work has to do with the outer person of either the teacher or disciple. And yet most practitioners believe it is the outer person rather than the real being of the teacher with whom they interact. This is the cause of so much misunderstanding, and yet the outer form of the teacher also has a part to play.

As has belonged to so much of my experience of the path, this paradoxical relationship between the human and the Divine is at the center of the relationship with the teacher. I have personal faults and failings like anyone, and yet I have been trained, been made empty, to hold a transmission of love that is pure and impersonal. Because this pure love goes directly from heart to heart, it creates a feeling of intimacy that evokes needs, projections, and misunderstandings in the disciple. The journey of the disciple is of necessity through this maze of misunderstandings created by the divine love that comes through the teacher. Without the human presence of the teacher this drama would not take place, and yet it is due to the emptiness within the teacher that the wayfarer is drawn into this labyrinth, and hopefully, finally, into the mystery of merging, when human and divine reveal their essential unity.

COMMITMENT

When I first began this work I traveled around America giving lectures and workshops, finding the people who belonged to this Sufi path.[42] It was a miracle to suddenly feel this love within my heart connecting with another, to experience its sweetness and the sense of a tradition coming alive. What had begun in a room in North London was now present in lecture halls and living rooms across North America, like an ancient promise or a dream being answered. And my heart and life were a part of this promise, this mystery of love being awakened. An outer journey of so many motel rooms and rental cars was mirrored by an inner journey that brought a deep joy and sense of fulfillment. Even after twenty years I still find it a miracle when I see an unfamiliar face across a lecture room and find that he or she is already in my heart, or when I hear a dream that carries the ancient imprint of the path, discover a young man whose journey has taken him years and many miles to find his way here, and know that he is now where he belongs.

Over the years gradually more people were drawn to this path, and meditation groups formed in different parts of the world. For some strange reason North America, northern Germany, Switzerland, and London have become the places most people following this path are gathered.[43] Outwardly we meet in these places, in the format of a lecture, a seminar, or weekly meditation groups. Inwardly we are present within the circle of love that belongs to this Sufi path, the mysterious gathering of souls on the inner planes where the real work takes place. The people following the path have become like a family. I know their lives, the joys and sorrows of their children, the demands of their work. I have heard their stories and know the longing that has always been present.

Only as the years passed did I come to realize the sense of responsibility and commitment that are involved in this work of the soul. Much is said about the need for commitment on the part of the wayfarer: without commitment there can be no progress along the path. Less understood is the depth of commitment on the part of the teacher. Without this complete commitment the disciple can easily be left stranded between the worlds, unable to return to a former ego-identity, yet lacking the energy or guidance needed to cross into the deeper reality of the Self. The teacher has to take responsibility for the disciple, whatever their limitations, doubts, or inner resistance. The disciple can hesitate, even step off the path. Disciples have this freedom. But the teacher has to remain committed to the potential the wayfarer has for the journey, hold the truth of her inner light even when it is obscured. The teacher has to follow an ancient code of practice that gives the wayfarer the best opportunity to make the journey, to live their longing for God. Rarely does the disciple understand what is being offered, or the price that the teacher has to pay to keep this connection of love alive. Only if the disciple behaves unethically or makes a conscious decision to no longer follow a spiritual life is the commitment of the teacher withdrawn, the link between their hearts broken.

The wayfarer who is drawn onto the path of love will make many mistakes, and through the drama of projection and misunderstanding may get angry with the teacher, feel abandoned, even at times betrayed. In the East these feelings were contained within the tradition of *adab*, the correct behavior to have in the presence of the teacher. But in the West not only do we not have the real practice of *adab*; we have a culture that encourages the self-expression of the ego and has no understanding of what is really involved on the spiritual path. Often as a teacher I have had to accept the anger, resentment, even hostility of individuals faced with the darkness within themselves. So many times I have been blamed for inner problems or outer difficulties. One has to be trained in detachment or have the gift of compassion at such times to remain true to the highest potential of the disciple and not react. To wait with patience for weeks, or even sometimes years, until the darkness dissolves and the higher light within the disciple shines through. In these times to even want the wayfarer to progress or change is an obstacle. The disciple must be left free to make mistakes and experience her darkness. Sometimes, much later, the disciple may be made aware of how she has behaved. Sometimes it is never even mentioned. This is the tradition.

TRUST AND DISTRUST

As a teacher I have to trust the light within the disciple and the knowing that the path will nurture and guide this light, will take it where it needs to go. It is not that "I" know, but I have deep faith in the path itself, in this Sufi system that has been guiding souls Home for centuries. And I have faith in my sheikh who has trained me in a way that enables my light to be used in this work. For hundreds of years seekers have been coming to the path with their longing and difficulties, and this tradition has embraced them. There is a deep wisdom in the path itself: so many souls, so many difficulties, and yet the path remains as a living force. I trust that we are each given what we need, even if it is not in the way we want or expect. Real spiritual life is always so different from any expectations.

Yet in America I have encountered a difficulty that has taken me years to understand, and that is a cultural disrespect for real spiritual work and any real spiritual tradition.[44] This deep disrespect appears to be a part of our Western mind and psyche, and can subtly undermine the work of the path. It is as if there is a deep cultural distrust of giving oneself to a spiritual path. This is easy to understand if it is the result of a recent experience with cults or some other form of spiritual abuse, but I sense that it goes deeper than that. Maybe it comes from an early Puritan imprint that was an escape from any imposed religious dogma. Maybe it is simply because the West—and in particular America—does not have any esoteric spiritual traditions as a part of its heritage, and distrusts something its does not understand, especially something that cannot be bought with money. Or maybe it is because America has sold its spiritual principles for material prosperity, and so has lost its own self-respect. Whatever the reason, this disrespect runs deep within the collective, and can easily poison the attitude of the wayfarer. Its presence is particularly felt when the way-farer encounters difficulties or apparent contradictions in relation to the path or the teacher. It is surprisingly easy to undermine this work of the soul.

In other cultures a spiritual teacher and a spiritual path are respected, even by those who do not follow them. Here in the West we are left with the debris of a dying materialistic culture that has long lost touch with the sacred. Our collective disrespect for the sacred and its traditions casts a shadow on our individual and world soul, blurring the brightness of our inner light, making it more difficult to recognize an inner truth. We do not trust what is real, preferring a spirituality that is subtly distorted, whose promises of enlightenment, if one looks closely, belong to the ego rather than the Self. We are more comfortable with what is false. And in this materialistic culture it is much easier to trust what can be bought or sold. A true spiritual path cannot be bought or sold, but like the sunlight is free.

I have learned that there is nothing to be gained from confronting this collective shadow, but it is important to recognize the forces that interfere with the work of the soul. Distrust and disrespect are subtle poisons that create distortions in the relationship between teacher and disciple. Regardless, my work is always to respect the light within the individual, and to trust that this light and the light of the path will guide the soul Home.

FROM HEART TO HEART

From heart to heart the transmission of love is given, the love that the wayfarer needs to make the journey. "The disciple progresses through love. Love is the driving force, the greatest Power of Creation. As the disciple has not enough love in him to have sufficient of the propelling power to reach the Goal, so love is increased, or 'created' simply by activating the Heart Chakra."[45] The teacher activates the heart of the disciple, giving her the love that is needed. This is the grace of the tradition, the transmission of love without which the path would no longer be alive. In the Naqshbandi path there is a bond between teacher and disciple, *rābita*, that contains this link of love. It can be experienced as a special sweetness within the heart.

The transmission of love is given effortlessly, and, once the bond has been created, is automatic. It does not even need physical presence, but can be given on the inner plane of the soul when the disciple is asleep. The link of love exists beyond the limitation of time and space. When the love is needed it flows from heart to heart. The disciple may not even be consciously aware of what is given, but sometimes awakes with a feeling of sweetness, or even bliss, or a dream of being together with the teacher. Inwardly the teacher is always attentive, his heart attuned to the spiritual needs of the disciple.

It is as if the heart of the disciple is held within the heart of the teacher. As more and more people came to the path, I experienced my spiritual heart expanding to contain their hearts. They are a part of me, and the greater their longing, the more their desire for Truth, the closer I feel them to my spiritual center. They are always with me.

In the outer world the work of the teacher is to help the disciple stay true to the inner focus of the heart. Guidance may be needed to keep the inner or outer life aligned with the higher purpose of the soul, and also to deal with the difficulties that arise through this transmission of love. The love cleanses the heart and psyche, and often causes confusion to the mind. It is not easy to learn to live with the energy of divine love, as it has a vibration that is quicker than the density of our lower self and everyday consciousness. Transformation through love is a demanding process that requires inner attention and perseverance. We need to learn how to surrender to the love that is given and not to resist this higher power. Love can also create feelings of vulnerability and even anger as it triggers patterns of resistance or repressed inner pain. All these feelings need to come to the surface and be accepted and understood. Here the teacher can help the disciple to differentiate what belongs to the work of inner transformation from what is a distraction that can be avoided. It is easy to get caught in unnecessary inner dramas, and the distractions of the mind and psyche can be endless. We all bring our patterns of avoidance along with our desire for Truth.

On this path we also work with dreams that guide us, helping us to understand the inner work that needs to be done, the psychological blocks that may be an obstacle, the darkness we need to confront and accept. Dreams may also give us images of the mysterious process of inner transformation, of love's journey through the chambers of the heart. Some dreams are spiritual teachings or experiences on the plane of the soul that need to be understood from a solely spiritual perspective. Dreams are often shared within the meditation group, where they are given the interpretation that is needed. But what matters is always the attitude of the dreamer, whether one is able to listen and be open and receptive to the meaning of the dream, to the energy of its images. As a teacher I am sometimes given direct insight into the meaning of a dream, or I may just allow its meaning to surface through group discussion. I also need to be attentive to my own dreams, to the way the path reveals itself in my own psyche. The journey always continues.

LOVE'S DARK SIDE

There is also a dark side to this transmission of love. One afternoon my teacher sat me at her kitchen table and told me a strange story that shocked me. She told it to me three times so that I knew it was for me. It was the story of how they make a torturer: how someone is tortured and tortured until he is broken, and then he is taught how to torture others. There can be great cruelty to the workings of love, and sometimes the teacher is the instrument of this cruelty.

Most wayfarers are taken Home gradually through the simple power of love working within them, echoing the words of al-Hallāj, "When Truth has taken hold of a heart She empties it of all but Herself." Love and longing purify and transform us, emptying us of our self. But sometimes the ego is too strong to surrender and then the disciple needs to be broken. This is a terrible task for the teacher because the disciple is always dear to the teacher: the link of love holds him or her in your heart. But occasionally instructions are given from within the heart and this dark work of love begins.

It is a subtle process, hardly ever done with any outer show of anger, although sometimes that is necessary. We all have particular weaknesses within us, places where we are vulnerable and afraid. It is here that the teacher begins to pressure the disciple, usually with an energy of cold detachment that can seem heartless. A comment here, a remark there are often all that is needed; sometimes the disciple is simply seemingly ignored for months. There are many ways to break a human being in order to help them to make this step, and when there is great love between teacher and disciple the pain is particularly potent. My teacher called her sheikh her "beloved executioner," so often did he appear hard, cold, and distant to her.

You have to be trained to do this work. It is one of the most painful things anyone can be asked to do. And it is done with great love, a love that does not allow anything to get in the way on the road towards Truth. You can also only do this work if it has been done to you. It is the dark side of love, and a work that is much misunderstood. Something within the disciple is destroyed, torn out, crushed. They are broken, made empty.

Part of this process often manifests as an experience of feeling abandoned, betrayed by the teacher. The teacher may "put all the appearances against him; he will appear full of faults and all kinds of defects."[46] The disciple may be forced to abandon any images or projections he placed on the teacher, and often becomes angry, even hostile. He is not aware of the great love on the part of the teacher that is needed to do this work—the human being has to be broken with love; otherwise it could leave a terrible scar in the psyche and even the soul. It is all part of this ancient training, how a human being is destroyed and remade with love, so that he can contain the vaster dimension of Truth.

If the teacher were not completely surrendered he could easily interfere with this process, want to make it easier for the disciple, to help in the work. Then the breaking would not be complete and the pain would be wasted. The knife must be clean and cold, and although there is great love there is also an inhuman quality to this work. And yet I am not separate from this process. Although I have to put all my own feelings aside, still it hurts: it tears the fabric of my own heart.

THE DRAMA OF PROJECTION

It is easy to idealize the work of the teacher, of one who has been made "featureless and formless" by love so that this work can be done to others. When I sat at the feet of my teacher I was in awe of what she was given, of the power of Truth she carried within her. Yes, there are oceans of love to which one has access, and the grace of the tradition is always present or the work could not continue. But one is always given for others, never for oneself, and there is a human cost to this work that is rarely understood.

There is the simple burden of being responsible for the souls of others, of keeping open the doors of grace. One of the first things my teacher told me was that none of us are indispensible, and one is always aware of that. Even so, to carry the energy of the path and its teachings is a tremendous responsibility. This is not a nine-to-five job, and there are no weekends off! It is the job of the teacher to be inwardly with all of the disciples all of the time, to keep the inner attention awake. Although this is a spiritual work that takes place on the level of the soul, there is a human cost to being the focus of so many lives, so many aspirations, the central figure in so many dreams. There is a sacrifice that has to be made again and again as one's own life is lived in a state of surrender to the work. I first realized this when I lived above my teacher and saw the constant stream of people who came to her door. But in the last twenty years I have come to know for myself how subtly draining it can be. At times it takes me to the point of exhaustion. So many times something human within me rebels, and wants to be left alone. I have images of a small cottage in Scotland surrounded by the wild moors and the wind and the rain!

There is also this strange burden of projection. One not only carries the aspirations of the wayfarer, but also many strange projections, particularly in a culture that has no understanding of this tradition. One is the focal point of the inner life of the disciple, and everything one says or does not say is interpreted as deeply meaningful. One learns to be careful when speaking, knowing at the same time that most of what one says will be misunderstood. How can mystical truth be understood by the rational mind? The disciple looks through the veil of the ego and its conditioning. The reality of love is so different.

The disciple wants the teacher to be perfect, to be all-knowing, rather than just someone who has been made empty. I have learned that some people think I know their every thought, their hidden secrets and their future. They do not realize that I know nothing except when it is necessary to help the disciple to make a step or avoid an unnecessary difficulty. Why would I want to burden myself with so many thoughts? I am just used when I am needed. And sometimes when I am made to know something about a disciple, her inner or outer situation, I am not allowed to share it with her, even if I think it may help. She has to be free to walk her own way, make her own mistakes.

It is very easy to get caught in the projections of others, to become a helper, savior, or even their image of a teacher. As every therapist knows, an individual person's projections can be very strong. The projections of a spiritual group are a thousand times more powerful, particularly one full of people who have done many years of meditation, whose inner focus as a result is stronger. One has to be very attentive not to try to live up to their expectations but rather to take the ground out from under those expectations whenever possible, while always maintaining one's detachment. Although the disciple is free to project what she wants onto me, I have to want nothing again and again. I cannot even react against the projections, as this would engage me in their drama.

Sometimes I think that although I have tasted the real freedom of surrender, those who are just walking the path are in many ways more free than I am. They are free to make mistakes and forget, to put aside the work of the path for their own reasons, even get lost in the world from time to time. I am bound to be always attentive, to hold the light regardless of how I may feel. I cannot abandon the disciple, even though the disciple is free to abandon or even betray the path.

But at the same time I am given that deepest joy of seeing and experiencing a human being awakened to the Divine and making the journey Home. When I hear dreams or experiences that reflect that ancient journey I feel deeply touched to be a part of this process, a witness or participant in these stories of divine love. Every human being is so infinitely precious, but a person who has been touched by the tenderness or fire of real love has a special sweetness. It is often those one would least expect who make the serious steps on the path, who become lost in deep states of meditation or feel the presence of divine oneness. And to know that one has played a small part in this awakening, even as just a witness, is deeply nourishing. I know that it is all due to the grace of my sheikh and the energy of the path, but something in me has been present as a soul turns towards God, or when that light is lit within the heart. There is nothing one wants more than for another to taste the Truth that is at the root of all.

And sometimes one is given the privilege of preparing a disciple for physical death, for that last journey. Then one can see almost visibly how the grace works, how the individual is given the experiences that she needs in order to complete this life, and how she can become free from any inner or outer attachments that might impede her journey beyond this world. One friend was given the direct experience of life that she had never had. Her cancer went into unexpected remission for two years, and as she walked the beaches near her home or watched the sunsets, she was at last able to be present with life in a simple and pure way, free of all the dramas of self that had dominated her life. Life and its joy were present in their essence. Another friend was able to go in a state of infinite sweetness and tenderness, with a presence in her room that carried this fragrance of love. Her eyes had already seen the other side before she died. Mostly the work of the teacher is to help the disciple to "die before you die," to become free of the ego with all its patterns of attachment while still in this world. But sometimes one can help in this more final transition, as life's journey is fulfilled through love.

BURNOUT

I could not do any of this work without the constant inner help of my sheikh. How could I carry the burden of a disciple's aspirations on my own, without real support? At the beginning he was always present in my meditations, giving me advice and answering my questions. He also showed me when I made a mistake, and helped me to correct it. But over the years he has left me more and more alone, unless there is a real need that I cannot answer. I have had to stand on my own feet in the shifting sands of this world, knowing that although his energy is present I have to make my own decisions. I trust in his trust of me, but sometimes it is a very lonely, heart-wrenching business. I have been given much outer help, especially from my wife, whose feminine wisdom and understanding and deep connection to the path have been an invaluable support. And yet at the same time I am left more and more with my own humanness and imperfections. I no longer aspire to anything, not even to be a better teacher. The work seems to have washed everything out of me.

Partly this inner state came as a result of what I can only describe as a spiritual burnout that began some years ago, after I had been doing this work for over fifteen years. For fifteen years I had pushed myself, lecturing and being with people, as slowly over the years more and more people came with their mixture of spiritual longing and human dramas. During this time I discovered that I could give people a certain light to help them, to help to free them from inner blocks and align them with their higher Self and their true purpose. After I had spent time with a person in this way the light was drained out of me, but then in meditation it would be replenished. Although I would often be tired, there was always enough light.

Usually it seemed to be the everyday difficulties that dominated people's consciousness and to which I was pushed to respond—problems with work or relationships. Rarely were there real questions about the inner relationship with God. At the same time my own journey was drawing me further and further into the emptiness, into the formlessness beyond creation. How could I help people with problems about this world when my inner attention was being turned elsewhere, into a dimension far distant from the ego and its concerns? I felt inadequate to answer their questions, to understand their problems that, although real and pressing to them, to me appeared insubstantial.

It became harder and harder for me to hold the light of their spiritual aspiration in the midst of these demands. I do not know whether spiritual work has always been like this, or whether the collective darkness and forget-fulness in the West have emphasized this—whether the individual light now is more easily caught in the collective darkness, a darkness that also carries a self-obsession with the ego-self and its endless problems. I began to feel more and more drained. I tried to say that I could only work with people's spiritual self and not their psychological dramas. I even stopped interpreting dreams for a while. But I realized that it is almost impossible to separate the personal and spiritual, that the individual path is lived through our human drama and its apparent difficulties. I had to accept and work with people as they were. But I felt my own light and life force being more and more drained, less easily replenished, until finally I had little left to give.

The energy of the path still came through me, but I had also discovered that often it needed a human con-tainer, that on its own it was too inhuman, too detached for people to easily digest. It needed the container of my own human nature, and yet that was getting more and more exhausted. And then there was the added difficulty of working in the United States after the invasion of Iraq, with the collective darkness that the invasion constellat-ed. As many people know, after 9/11 there was a period of grace when the prayers of millions around the world were turned toward the United States. Yet this grace did not last and the invasion of Iraq triggered a cloud of darkness that all but obscured the spiritual sun. Spir-itual work in the U.S. became much more difficult and demanding over these years, as individuals were con-fronted not only by their personal darkness but also by this collective shadow.[47] Holding the light in these times drained almost all my reserves, until finally I could not continue. I was "burned out" and for over a year I was physically ill.

That time has passed and my physical health returned. That shadow over the United States has gradually lifted. But something has changed. The light is different. A spark that had been present when I first came to America is no longer here. And I know that I will never be able to work with people in the same way again. I can no longer afford to give them my own spiritual light to help them on their journey. I have enough light to stay attuned to the energy of the path and to ensure that its grace be given where it is needed. But those years of darkness took with them a certain light from within me that has not been returned. This bewildered me for a long time. I suppose that means that this light is not needed, that I no longer need to help people in the same way. We each have to stand on our own feet, live our own light. Often I am reminded of Buddha's words to Ananda, his closest disciple, before he died:

> Therefore O Ananda,
> Take thyself for a light
> Take thyself for a refuge
> Never seek for a refuge in anyone else
> And work on thy salvation diligently.

We are all a part of the one light. Teacher, disciple, and path are just different reflections of the same one light as it comes into the world. And as the world shifts on its axis of love so the light within the world changes. Sufism has always adapted to the changing need of the time, and now we need to subtly adapt in the way we work, the way we are present in the light of the world.

When I was first sent to America to teach I came with an innocence and enthusiasm I no longer have. I have had to mature and understand more deeply what it means to guide people on this journey of the soul. I have seen more clearly the difficulties and demands of this work, as well as experiencing the deep joy of being present as love awakens and transforms the heart and life of another. But I have also come to see that our individual journey is part of a greater journey—the evolution of the whole. Nothing is separate. And I have seen that changes are taking place within this larger picture that affect the way we live our longing. The path will always continue, sometimes more hidden, sometimes more visible. And the relationship of teacher and disciple will also continue—the mysterious transmission of love from heart to heart. And yet something has changed that is too far-reaching to fully understand at this moment. A certain light has been withdrawn and a certain light is waiting to be given. The soul of the seeker and the soul of the world are being drawn together more closely: a global oneness is coming nearer to our consciousness.[48] I am waiting to see how this light will work, both in the individual and in the whole. And I am trying to stay attuned to the currents of love as they come into the world. At the same time something within me has been washed away: some sense of what it means to be a teacher has gone. Maybe some new understanding will be born, or maybe this is just part of the deepening emptiness that belongs to this work.

5

Who Makes the Journey?

Meditating on the paradoxes of my inner experiences and the drama and difficulties of being a teacher, I have found hints and suggestions within the stories and writings of the Sufi tradition that explore the central paradox of the mystical path—that only God exists and there is nothing to arrive at, and yet there still seems to be a journey, and still an "I" who seems to need to make it. In particular I have been drawn to the description of the quest told by Farīd al-Dīn 'Attār in The Conference of the Birds, *which takes the reader through the seven valleys of the heart's journey, leading finally to the Valley of Poverty and Nothingness, "the nothingness of love." Who makes that journey? In this nothingness does anything remain?*

He had but one purpose in bringing forth
both worlds' Existence.
To see Himself in the mirror of the soul and then
to become the lover of Himself
who is without flaw.[49]

'Ayn'l-Qudāt Hamadhānī

ON THE HUMAN STAGE spiritual life circles around the drama of "I" and "Thou," the ego's relationship with the Self, the seeker's relationship with God. The practices and ethics of the path help us with the process of purification so that we can see our true nature more clearly, access our higher Self more directly. Gradually our consciousness becomes more aligned with the divine light within us, and this light flows more directly into our life. We make the slow and painful transition from a life solely directed by the ego, its desires and unconscious patterns, to a life under the protection and guidance of our divine nature, the Self. On most paths this is the work of a lifetime, requiring commitment and perseverance, as well as the grace that is given. Even though it often appears that all of our efforts are of little effect, as the ego and the patterns within our psyche seem to continually dominate us, something within the wayfarer changes—lead is turned into gold. This inner alchemical *opus* is the most deeply rewarding work we can do. It is the work of the soul in this world, the quest for the pearl of great price that we discover within our own self.

And yet this is only one facet of what we call spiritual life. It is essentially the work of inner transformation as seen from the perspective of the ego, of the one who sets out upon the journey. In 'Attār's parable of the quest, *The Conference of the Birds*, many different birds set out upon this journey and travel through various tests and tribulations. Finally the thirty birds who survive discover the radiance of "their own unique reality." This is the realization of one's true Self:

> Though you have struggled, wandered,
> travelled far,
> It is yourselves you see and what you are.[50]

But then "their Lord" reveals a further secret of the journey:

> How much you thought you knew and saw;
> but you
> Now know that all you trusted was untrue.
> Though you traversed the Valley's depths
> and fought
> With all the dangers that the journey brought,
> The journey was in Me, the deeds were Mine—
> You slept secure in Being's inmost shrine.[51]

That the journey itself is just another illusion is one of the most shocking spiritual secrets. At the beginning, when the heart is awakened, the traveler makes the decision to turn away from the illusions of the world to seek the reality found within. The turning of the heart is a turning from illusion towards Truth, and the traveler pays the price for this journey, as we leave behind many of the attachments and false identities that belong to the life of the ego. The traveler has to trust the path followed, the guidance that is given. But finally awakens to the deeper truth that even the journey itself is an illusion, that the "dangers" and difficulties encountered were not real. The price and the pain that needed to be paid were as unreal as the illusions left behind. What then is real?

"The journey was in Me, the deeds were Mine." The greatest journey of self-discovery, the journey into the darkness within oneself and beyond into the light of one's true being, was God's journey within Himself. Even our darkest moments of despair, the depths of our longing, the wasteland of desolation, were just another dream. "You slept secure in Being's inmost shrine." This simple truth is so primal as to be almost overwhelming. It was never about us.

When we take our first step on the journey we are told that we have to leave our self behind. In the words of Bāyezīd Bistāmī, "I saw my Lord in my dreams and I asked, 'How am I to find You?' He replied, 'Leave yourself and come!'" This seems like a simple statement of the renunciation of the ego, and this is how the journey appears. In Sufism this is the process of *fanā*, the annihilation of the ego that belongs to the arena of the heart, where like gladiators of old we salute our Emperor with the words *Morituri te salutant* (those about to die salute thee). As our ego is dissolved in the sweetness of love, or is pierced with love's sword, we sense a wonder that is waiting for us. We dream of a dawn that is coming, have visions of a light so bright it does not cast a shadow. And we know that this sacrifice of our ego, our "I," is our greatest offering, the most complete giving of our self. We do not dare to realize that this most painful process, this "dying before you die" is also a dream, that everything that belongs to the ego, even its "death," is an illusion.

If the journey itself is just a dream, then who or what finally awakens? Is this a secret we will ever know or understand? 'Attār writes:

No stranger followed them, or could unfold
The secrets they to one another told—
Alone at last, together they conferred;
Blindly they saw themselves and deaf they heard—
But who can speak of this? I know if I
Betrayed my knowledge I would surely die.[52]

'Attār here hints at the underlying secret of creation, the primal unity of the Divine, the oneness that is at the core of all mystical experience. The greatest illusion is not just that we exist as a separate, individual self, the "I," or even that we are separate from God, but that there is anything that is not God. As something within the mystic awakens to this knowing, we begin to participate in God's self-revelation—out of the appearance of duality and multiplicity comes an awakening to divine oneness. But it is never the seeker who awakens to oneness—this is just another illusion. It is God's awakening as God sees the oneness and multiplicity of the divine creation through the eye of our heart.

ONENESS AND MULTIPLICITY

Every atom of creation is a direct manifestation and expression of divine oneness. In creation's multiplicity there is only divine oneness revealing itself in different ways, each manifestation a different, unique expression of the Divine. In the words of Shāh Ne'matollāh:

> How wonderful that a single Essence should
> Refract itself like light, a single source
> Into a million essences and hues.[53]

And we are a part of this revelation. Our individual consciousness is a unique expression of divine consciousness. The uniqueness of our existence is a mirror of God's unique existence. This is the secret we carry within us, of which our heart can become conscious. And in this knowing we claim our deepest heritage as human beings. We are alive with the secret that is at the very core of creation, that is the light of a million suns.

What we call the "Journey Home" is a journey in which this divine secret is awakened into consciousness here in this world. God affirms divine unity within the apparent world of multiplicity. In the midst of this dream the light of Truth awakens. This is the mystery in which we participate, the secret for which we gave our life.

But what is this world into which we awaken? If all we know is a world of illusion, what is a world of Truth? Divine awareness in this world is very simple—direct experience. When we taste the strawberry, see the homeless man on the street, hear the cry of a child without the intercession of thought or judgment, then for an instant we are present in the world. This is the moment of Zen *satori*, when we go beyond the duality of thought into the eternal present, the moment that is. There is no "I" that intercedes, that veils us from the world as it really is, and for an instant we are awake. We also find our self present in a world that is awake. And it is a very different world than that created by our mind and its many images, by our psyche and our prejudices.

The images we see in this moment may appear to be the same as in our ego-filled existence, but they are completely different. The same strawberry is sweet, the same child cries, but in the moment of what is real there is an intensity, a clarity to what is so ordinary. The moment is fully alive, and we are not an observer, but an active participant, present in a dynamic instant that is unique, never to be repeated. In this instant the world is created anew and we belong to this creation. We are in the garden of creation, unadorned, in the primal simplicity of what is. It carries the mystery of what the Sufis call the secret of the word *"Kun!"* ("Be!").

This moment belongs to the real wonder of being alive, like the round red ball of the sun breaking through an early morning mist. Something comes alive for the first time as the Divine unveils Itself. We awake to the morning that is always present, even if it is hardly noticed, rarely seen. Life continues on its busy course, our mind comes back with its thoughts, but for that moment we were with the sunlight on the street, the joy of a spring of water breaking free from the ground.

And sometimes, in such a moment, we may glimpse something else: the light that belongs to God. Everything, every particle in creation, is surrounded by and infused with divine light. We do not see it because we are veiled by our own darkness and forgetfulness, but it is the light of creation remembering its Creator, or the light of the Creator's own self-expression—the brush stroke of the Great Artist. This light carries the alchemy of creation: it is the *spirit mercurius* alive in this world. It is the miracle of rebirth that belongs to matter, in which matter celebrates the bond of love between the Creator and the creation. It is matter alive with the presence of the Divine. And sometimes we are allowed to see this mystery, to see this dancing light. We cannot say it is like this or like that, because it has no comparison. Our mind cannot understand it even if our heart knows it is in the presence of something full of wonder. Once we have seen it we can never forget the real nature of matter. We can never think that matter is not alive.

Maybe, one day, this light will take humanity by the hand and lead it from the world of illusion to the Truth that is all around us. Maybe it will remind us that we never left the garden of Paradise—that it was just our own mind and ego that banished us. We will know directly that all of creation is both lead and gold. Until then it serves to remind us of the world that belongs to God.

THE DIVINE STORY

And this is only a part of the story. We are so used to being identified with our own story, our own journey, that it is easy to forget that the whole world is a continual telling of God's story. In the light that belongs to the reality of God, we can begin to see this story that is the real book of life, the divine life, God's story:

When your heart sees Reality,
Then every atom of creation is a window of
His house.[54]

And we belong in this house and are a part of this story in ways we cannot imagine. We may try to imagine our own life, but we have few images to imagine God's life or how our life belongs to the life of the Divine.

At the foundation of our life is the secret of divine oneness, and this is expressed in the mysterious relationship between our individual consciousness and the Divine. Central to the existence of each of us is the sense of our own individuality—we are living our life. Western civilization has celebrated this individuality, giving us the rights of the individual and even encouraging us to follow our own dream. On the surface this focus on our separate individual self can be seen as the expression of an ego-driven culture that denies the oneness that belongs to all of life. However, at its deepest, most sacred level, the expression of individual consciousness is a manifestation of the uniqueness of the Divine. We each have the potential to live and celebrate God's uniqueness. "He never repeats Himself in the same form twice." Each snowflake is unique, each leaf is different, and through the vehicle of our individual consciousness the Divine can have a unique experience of Its world.

From outer space we may see that the world is a single whole, but through the consciousness of the individual the Divine can have millions of unique experiences of Its world. God is always one, but celebrates that oneness in the multiplicity of creation, the multitude of unique experiences of life—"You show Your face every moment in a thousand mirrors, in every mirror You show Your face differently."[55] Once we remember that it is God's life we are experiencing, we can consciously participate in this divine revelation. We can be present and celebrate the moment that *is*.

But who is this "I" who has the experience? And what is its relationship to the Divine that encompasses everything? In the deepest place within the heart there is no "I," but a merging in which all is lost in the vastness of the Divine. There is the blinding light that belongs to God and is the source of all that exists. And the light of our consciousness, that precious light that gives us our existence, is not separate from the intensity of God's light. It may be veiled by "seventy thousand veils of light and seventy thousand veils of darkness" but it is still the same light. Human consciousness has the capacity to be a microcosm of a vaster consciousness. This is the unique potential of the human being in the whole spectrum of existence: "we are made in the image of God."

At the beginning of the spiritual journey we know our own existence; we have a sense of our self—even if later we discover that it is just an illusory self, a persona, an ego-identity. But once the journey has completely claimed us we only know that we have lost all sense of self; we have been consumed like the moth in the flame. What remains can only be God:

If you lose yourself
 on this path
you will know in certainty:
 He is you, you are He.[56]

This is the secret for which many mystics have been killed, the heresy for which they have been sacrificed. And yet it is the primal truth underlying human consciousness. Our light is God's light, because how can there be two? The mystic even comes to know that the veils that create the illusion of separation are God's veils. In the words of Ibn 'Arabī: "We are veiled from Thee only through Thee, and Thou art veiled from us through Thy manifestation."[57]

At the beginning of the journey we may see an illusory world through the eyes of an illusory self. But as we are drawn into the mystery of the heart something within us is awakened that can perceive and experience a world of Truth. What is awakened is divine consciousness, which alone can see what is Real. Through the heart of the lover the Beloved incarnates into His own world and experiences the love affair of creation that belongs only to God. It is all God's mysterious drawing back of divine veils— God coming to know divine oneness through a human being. This belongs to the essence of the path, the journey from our existence to God's existence.

And yet, there is no journey and no traveler, because only God exists. Everything else is a dream. The journey, the traveler, the process of transformation—it is all a dream. And when something within us awakens from this dream there is only laughter, even if we cried so many tears on the way. With this laughter comes a deep understanding, a knowing that points towards a divine purpose: what God is writing in the book we call the world.

6

A Human Story
in a Divine Drama

This next chapter, adapted from the second edition of my spiritual autobiography, The Face Before I Was Born, *explores from my own personal perspective how the very idea of a spiritual journey has changed for me in the forty years since I set out upon the path. So many expectations have been left behind, lost, and often I wonder what is really left. There is a journey and yet I sense that it was never my journey. Something more enduring has surfaced than could ever belong to me. Mystical life is a process of losing rather than finding, and yet through this losing something is revealed. I also sense that however much has changed within me, has been dissolved, abandoned, a simple human quality has remained.*

OVER TEN YEARS HAVE passed since I wrote my spiritual autobiography, *The Face Before I Was Born*, which told the tale of my initial years on the path, the story of my first experiences of meditation and how they drew me to a teacher and deep within myself. Reading it now I can recognize the person who wrote it: I can remember some of the feelings, the traumas, the beauty, and the love. And yet it appears to me now as fundamentally the story of another person, of a fragmented self struggling to find something, to uncover and claim a deeper meaning. Yes, the journey took me to a sense of wholeness, to a deep coming together as psychological conflicts came to the surface and began to be reconciled. But little did I know ten years ago that this journey was just the beginning, and that the real pilgrim is not the person whose story was told.

In *The Face Before I Was Born* I told as honestly as I could the story of my spiritual journey as it appeared then. And this journey took me home, back to what was real and essential within myself. The book tells the story of a seeker being slowly stripped naked, the painful process of the clothes of conditioning and self-image being removed. This spiritual uncovering is real and painful, and is a necessary journey—the journey to discover your real nature, "the face you had before you were born." But later one realizes that from the very beginning it was not about oneself. The deeper journey, the more real story, is how the light of the real Self pushes itself through into consciousness, demands to make itself known.

It is of course much easier to tell "our" story, our emotional, psychological, and spiritual journey, painful and intoxicating, demanding and tremendously rewarding. It is very difficult to realize that essentially it is not about us, that within our human drama a deeper drama is taking place, as the Divine finds ways to bring Itself into consciousness, to be born again. Sometimes the Divine works through subtlety and cunning, deceiving us into allowing It into our life, using the whole image of the spiritual journey as a sly contrivance to draw us into a divine mystery, to enable That which is Real to be born in us and into the world. And sometimes It comes with violence and seeming cruelty, forcing us to step aside, striking like lightning.

And yet few words can be said about this deeper journey, this real birth. Our language, our images, even our feelings belong to the ego and its relationship to the world. They help us understand *our* place in the world and *our* life's journey. The Divine, that eternal presence which is always here and yet continually reveals Itself anew, is a mystery beyond words, something that can be hinted at but hardly told. Looking back now on the story I wrote ten years ago of my journey, I feel more clearly the presence of that Other. I sense Its light behind the incidents and happenings of the way, how It was pushing me to make Itself known—the real story of the journey, which I only glimpsed in the last pages of my book.

There is also an innocence to this spiritual story as I told it there which I no longer have. Since writing that book my teacher, Irina Tweedie, died, and as her sheikh said to her, many things are revealed only after the teacher's death. When I wrote my autobiography I still believed in the spiritual journey as something to be accomplished, a journey with a destination. And so I experienced the "events" of the story through this image of a journey Home, a journey which I traveled with all of my longing and struggles. I now know that the journey was just an image, something that gave me a certain security and belonging, a sense of purpose. But the Divine does not belong to our images—we cannot imprison It within our beliefs or concepts. How all of my spiritual images were destroyed, how even the journey itself was tossed aside, is a story too painful for me to tell at this time. But I have lost my spiritual innocence in ways I could never have imagined, and I am left with a sense as much of human fragility as of divine grandeur, light, and glory. There is laughter when I write this, but tears are also very near. The relationship between the human and divine, and how they are one, is one of life's primal secrets.

The human drama is real in its pain and bliss, but this is only one facet of something so remarkable, so wonderful and so terrible. Once the clothes of "you" and "I" have been taken or torn off, there can be a glimpse of another drama, Another's story. And yet in many ways this is also our own story, for what are we but a spark of the Divine, and what is our journey but this spark being born into human consciousness, becoming a fire? The real mystery is how It unveils Itself within us; how the

Beloved makes Himself known to Himself in the fragile container of the human being.

And yet there is also something profoundly beautiful about the part we have to play in this process, the human side of the divine drama. I had hoped that the human being, the "I," would dissolve completely, the moth lost in the flame. And yet although there have been inner experiences of complete dissolving, being lost so completely it would appear that nothing could ever be found again, each time there has been a return to something essentially human, some segment of self. This particle is very different from the fragmented human being who began the journey those years ago, and yet at the same time there is an essential similarity, as if it carries the same unique stamp. The meaning of this return, the part the human plays in this divine unfolding, seems to be one of the great mysteries.

In the years since writing my autobiography I have felt more strongly both the power of the divine and the human qualities, which are transient, almost evanescent, and yet so necessary for this mystery to unfold. What is the real nature of the human being in the midst of the divine drama? We know only too well human nature as it struggles to survive and how it so easily follows the paths of greed and desire. We see the ravages of this around us in our polluted and desecrated world. But what are the human qualities that belong to the divine drama? What do we bring to this marriage? I do not attempt to understand fully this question, one that has haunted me for many years. I know in every cell the intensity of the Divine and the need to bow down before It. But there is something within the human being that is needed for Its revelation, for the mystery of divine incarnation. Maybe as I look back at those early years and see the struggle and longing, the despair and craziness, I can sense that my very human failing was an important partner. Possibly this is what we really have to offer: our inadequacies, our limitations, our longing.

'Attār tells a story of the great Sufi, Bāyezīd Bistāmī: "He called to me in my innermost interior: 'Oh Bāyezīd. Our treasure chambers are filled with approved deeds of obedience and pleasing acts of worship. If you want Us, offer up something which We don't have!' I said: 'What is it that You don't have?' The voice said: 'Helplessness and impotence, need and humility and a broken spirit.'"

In the midst of the drama of divine revelation there is a human story to be told. This is not a hero's tale and there is no spiritual ladder of ascent. What I saw as a spiritual quest I now sense to be closer to a partnership, in which we discover those qualities the Beloved wants and needs, those very human failings that are close to His heart. In this relationship we are nothing, a piece of dust blown on the floor. And yet it would seem we are also close to our Beloved's heart, infinitely precious.

7

Meditation and the "I"

Meditation has been my central spiritual practice and it has taken me far beyond the ego into love's light and darkness where there is nothing and no one. More and more I have come to experience the illusory, insubstantial nature of the ego, and yet, paradoxically it has remained. Returning from meditation it is always present. And so I have been haunted by the question of its purpose. I have come to feel that its illusory nature itself may hold a truth that is hidden in the blinding light or overwhelming darkness of the Divine.

There where the waves
of the endless sea are crashing
how should the Ocean hobnob
with a little dewdrop?

Fakhruddīn 'Irāqī [58]

THE JOURNEY BEYOND THE "I"

I first sat in meditation when I was sixteen. I closed my eyes and found myself in a reality beyond the mind and its images. I was present in a formless inner world completely different from the closed world of my schoolboy adolescent consciousness. Here there was endless inner space and freedom, a sense of deep inner expansion. There were no thoughts, nothing to look for or escape from. This was my first taste of a reality beyond the "I" and it remained when I[59] came back from meditation. My sense of schoolboy self returned, but something else was also present. A light and quality of space were visible. It was especially tangible when I was alone in nature, when instead of feeling caught in the confines of my boarding school, something else was alive. The flowers, the birds, the trees sparkled, and when I sat by the river and watched the water flowing by I was present in a moment that before I had never known existed. At the time I was just immersed in this state. I did not think about it. Only much later, after its magic had faded, did I come to realize what I had been given. When there is no "I" there is no thought, but just the present moment alive in its intensity.

Gradually the space and the freedom that came from this initial experience faded, as happens for most of us after such a glimpse. And in its place there was a seeker, struggling to recapture what had been given. Meditation had taken me beyond the "I" and yet the "I" returned, and brought with it a desire to continue with meditation, to practice yoga, to study spiritual texts, to fast and pray. Instead of the simplicity of this original state, the light dancing on the water, there was a person pushing himself with all the drive of a young man. Yes, there were moments when I glimpsed as if behind the curtain, stopped and saw a spider's web glistening with early morning dew, but the "I" seemed always to want more, was unsatisfied. Even meditation became an effort, a daily discipline.

And so I drove myself, hungry, exhausted, full of images of spiritual life and how to live it, until one day an old woman's piercing blue eyes looked at me, and I became just a piece of dust on the floor. Once again there was no "I," not even a frightened young man, just a piece of dust. Nothing was given or taken away. It just was. The path was present in its purity and essence, "a piece of dust at the feet of the teacher."

And so again I sat and meditated. Meditated in my teacher's small room and at home. This was a different meditation practice, a different path. Rather than meditating on emptiness it was a meditation on love, in which one drowns the mind in the energy of love within the heart. I meditated for hours. But once again there was struggle and effort, trying to still the chatter of the mind, trying to be present in love. Even the body rebelled, did not like me to sit still. There was no bliss, not even peace.

Looking back I could laugh at it all, if I did not still remember the pain and struggle, the longing and tears. Meditation, which could take me beyond the "I," instead seemed to have created a supercharged sense of self, charged with all the desire for spiritual truth. I struggled to seek what before had been given. Now I know that the ego, even a spiritual ego, cannot realize what is beyond the ego. Then I only knew the impatience and effort of my own intention. I was stuck with a young man's spiritual self.

And so began the drama of the path. The self that wants is also the self that obstructs. And meditation was a doorway into a world beyond the self. Imperceptibly, week after week, it sowed the seeds of my own destruction. Taking me into my heart, it gave me the sense of what it was like to be lost in love, to be drowned in that sweetness that was before honey or bee. Of course it was not always like this. There were days when there was only the cycle of my own thoughts which I struggled to leave behind, thoughts that caught my attention, seemed at that moment so important. But the meditation and the love were working their magic, slowly dissolving me. And then the states of *dhyana* began and I was lost to the world and lost to myself.

On this Sufi path the meditation of the heart drowns the mind in the energy of love within the heart, until finally the mind stops, absorbed in the love. This is the state of *dhyana*, where there is no mind, no consciousness, no individual self. It can seem like sleep but it is not sleep, because even in sleep the mind is present, creating dreams. In the state of *dhyana* there are no

147

dreams. There is nothing. It is said that the individual consciousness is absorbed into the universal consciousness. But I knew nothing, except that after half an hour, or longer, I returned. I knew only that I had been absent. There were moments before being drawn into *dhyana* when my mind was afraid, frightened of an emptiness where it did not exist. But finally the mind would dip, become lost, absorbed, and nothing remained. It is said that this is the first real taste of the Truth that is beyond the mind. But all I knew was that I was not present.

Each day I was allowed a certain time for meditation. I could close the door of my room and my children, who were young at the time, knew not to disturb me. For those sweet, empty minutes I could be lost, be nowhere, nothing. No consciousness, except that sometimes I returned from these states with a sense that I had been taken. Looking back, I see it was a time of pure wonder in unknowing, unbeing. I would start meditation, go into the heart, feel the currents of love begin to move, and then I would return some time later. Once again I would see the world around me, once again experience being myself. It was not a dramatic experience, because how can what is *not* be dramatic? But there was a sense of being where I belonged, even though there was no "I" and no experience.

And so the years passed. Through these states of *dhyana* a certain intensity of the path faded, until one day I had a dream in which I saw a coffin on which was written "Spiritual Aspirant." I then knew that one stage of the journey in which I was a seeker was over. There was no longer any spiritual aspiration. The seeker had died. In the depths of myself I just became more lost, more drawn into the darkness that is beyond the mind. Who can say anything about what is not, except that there were moments when I began to sense, to bring into consciousness, this emptiness that is Real.

There were also other experiences in meditation, a love that was given that permeated every cell of my body. And out of meditation there were states of peace, a peace that had no outer cause, but was just present, sometimes for days. A depth of peace that also permeated my mind and body. These were passing states, and yet they change you, they give a foundation for an existence that does not belong to the ego, the "I." It was not that "I" was loved, but rather that love was present. "I" was not at peace; the peace was present, all around me and within me. And so slowly, gradually, from out of the depths of *dhyana* a consciousness arose that one could call the consciousness of the Self. For me, as for so many others, it was not dramatic, not a burst of light, no fireworks of spiritual awakening. But there was a dawning awareness of a sense of being that was me but not "I," not my normal ego-self. A consciousness with awareness but no thoughts. And it was this consciousness that began to grow within me.

The wonder of the path is how it happens of its own accord. Like the classical image of the lily opening its petals on the surface of the water, something opens within the heart. The Sufis call it the "eye of the heart." It has a stillness and silence to it, and it seems completely natural. And yet the ego was still present. At this time I was a schoolteacher, teaching English literature to adolescent girls. And then I became a student, working on my Ph.D., so I needed my mind. I needed my own opinions. My children were growing up and they needed me to be present, to play with them, read them stories, help them with their homework. And yet all this time this Other became more present, not always on the surface, but like a friend, a companion who has come to stay.

I still had problems, psychological difficulties, dreams, challenges. There were still tears to be cried, times of tension and stress. Life was all around in its darkness and light. And I did not really think about this inner shift. I just lived the states as they came and went, and sensed this growing Other. Sometimes it was all veiled from me, sometimes my ego just did not want to know. It did not really matter. The path takes you on its own journey. More and more you wonder what it has to do with "you." You are not just an onlooker, a bystander, because it involves the whole of you, every cell of your body, every breath you take. And yet it is not about you. Often much of the ego-self remains unchanged. I still had my English upbringing, many of my patterns of behavior. I even still had a desire for what I called "Truth." And yet at the same time I knew that it did not belong to me. And always there was this emptiness around my consciousness, this vaster dimension of non-existence that I felt at the borders of myself.

RETURNING TO THE EGO

Meditation took me deeper. Sometimes I would be conscious of leaving behind my ego-self with its daily worries and anxieties. I would feel myself being drawn into a space far beyond that small circle of consciousness. For a while I would be aware of the emptiness, even— paradoxically—be conscious of my own non-existence, before that would all be lost and there was no sense of self. I remember feeling how wonderful it was not to have a self, to be nothing, nowhere. It was the feeling of a deep and ancient fulfillment and freedom. I did not have to exist. Existence is so constricting, so limiting. There are such vast and wonderful spaces beyond. And we can live in this emptiness, really live, not just exist.

Sometimes I would return from these states slightly bewildered, not knowing where I had been taken. Once I remember coming back to the ego, as if returning to this planet from a long journey, and feeling my ego-self like an old suit of clothes encasing me as I reentered it, once again experiencing its anxieties and problems. Sometimes I did not want to come back, return to this constricted existence with its difficulties and misunderstandings. I had to discipline myself to come back, to return to my ordinary consciousness and the demands of outer life.

The states of meditation always change. Nothing is fixed or constant. But I could not live without that daily infusion of what is beyond the mind, without that clear light and primal emptiness that is beyond the ego. It is like taking a deep breath of air before diving back into the water. But there is a shadow-side to this inner emptiness. At times this world with its pettiness and demands can feel so confining, its dramas so unnecessary. One has to learn how to live with the limitations of the ego, not to get angry or upset when one feels caught in patterns or problems that become increasingly unreal. Paradoxically, this sense of the unreality of one's problems can sometimes make one more upset, more angry, as if one were caught in a fairground hall of mirrors without seeing the humor in it.

Also something strange begins to happen to the "I." After certain inner experiences you know that your ego is an illusion. It is not real. You have tasted of the truth of who you really are, the center of being that really belongs to you. And yet you have to live in this illusory self, wear its clothes like everyone else. You cannot walk naked in the streets of this world. In my early twenties, after some powerful inner experiences, I tried to live in a state of complete openness. But I was too vulnerable, too immersed in oneness—quite crazy. In daily life you need to retain a sense of a separate self. And so you keep the ego you always had, except for this one dramatic difference. It knows that it is not real, that it is just a fabricated identity.

Initially this can be very confusing for the ego. Before, it was the main actor in your life; now it is just a bit player, mostly repeating old lines. It no longer grips you so tightly, is no longer the center of your existence. You see its patterns, its failings and inadequacies more clearly. And something has changed: it is no longer so solid. It is as if it has holes in it that allow the light from another world to enter and permeate it.[60] There is also a longing to be related to as your real self, but sadly this rarely happens. You keep your ego-self to relate to others, to function in their world. And this is the self to which you return. I was very relieved to read the ninth-century Sufi Junayd describing this state:

He is himself, after he has not been truly himself. He is present in himself and in God after having been present in God and absent in himself. This is because he has left the intoxication of God's overwhelming *ghalaba* (victory), and comes to the clarity of sobriety.... Once more he assumes his individual attributes, after *fanā*.[61]

Junayd also describes a particular tension in this state of being both absent and present.[62] Many spiritual texts describe the journey from the ego to the Self, or from existence to non-existence. What happens afterwards, how the lover returns from the embrace with the Beloved, is not so well documented.[63]

For many years I hoped to arrive at a spiritual state in which my real Self lived as a permanent presence in the center of my everyday consciousness, the sole actor on the stage of my life. Maybe some wayfarers are able to always remain in this state of a simple and direct consciousness, where one just "is." But although there are many moments when I can rest in this consciousness, particularly when I am alone in nature, I have found that the ego also remains, sometimes wondering about its own existence even as it knows it does not really exist. It can even get more anxious than before, concerned about its identity. At times it even wants reassurance, to feel that it is needed, has a purpose. And yet when I turn inward in meditation it is left behind so quickly.[64] And also sometimes during the day when I am taken into a deeper consciousness, it seems hardly present.

What then is the real nature of this self that remains? For years I tried to go beyond the ego, to leave it behind on my journey towards Truth. But now, when it falls away so easily, when the nothingness beyond the mind can become present in an instant and even the idea of a journey has been lost, I have to relearn how to live with it. And I have to rediscover the meaning for its continued presence, to see that it is not just a cardboard cut-out figure who nods to neighbors, stands in the check-out line with a few groceries, and watches the evening news. More and more there is a sense that this left-behind self, this "I," is not just an obstacle, something to be dismissed or transcended, but it is also essential to my human experience.

THE LIGHT OF THE EGO

The true individuality of the ego, our "I," is born from the light of the Self, of our true nature. I first directly observed this as I saw my grandchildren develop, how from the undifferentiated oneness of their first awareness the ego was born, their will and sense of "I." And within the "I" was the light of the Self, a spark that gave them their sense of individual existence. I think that without the light of the Self we would not have any sense of individuality but would just live an instinctual, physical existence. This is the change I saw in the early years of my grandchildren, how this spark of pure light gave birth to their distinct sense of their own unique self. This spark of light combines with the denser instinctual nature and other earth energies[65] to help form the ego (to which all of the patterns of conditioning are gradually added, forming our personality and character)—the same ego which too easily separates us from the very light that is at our center. Later we have to reclaim this light. And yet without its presence we would never have an individual self, there would be no ego to transcend.[66]

The soul needs the ego to live its presence in this world. On the plane of the Self there is no differentiation, only oneness. I remember when I was twenty-three spending six months almost solely on the plane of the Self. There was no sense of time, no difference in place. I would sit in the same place for hours. Everything was the same oneness. The consciousness of the Self sees only with the pure light in which all is one, and you are that oneness. It is the ego that experiences the separateness of things. If our divine Self wants to have a unique experience in this world it needs the ego. It needs the eyes of duality to see what is light and what is dark. It needs the vision of multiplicity to see the many colors of this world.

Of course it is a great joy to return to this oneness, especially after a lifetime caught in the dramas of duality. The pure light of the Self is a great blessing after a world full of shadows. But the ego gives us a possibility of experience that is not present in the Self: it gives a very human dimension to our divine consciousness. In the many colors of life something becomes visible that is hidden from the single light of pure being.

In my own experience my ego together with my deeper self took me on a spiritual quest. This journey even took me far beyond the created world, far beyond the abode of the ego. But every morning when I awake, the ego is still here. And when I come out of the depths of meditation, the ego is the first to greet me. It is a puzzling predicament, but what I am left with is the feeling that there is deep meaning in the relationship between the ego and the Self, between the drop and the ocean. And this relationship contains within it a secret of what it means for me to be a human being.

But who is this "I" who is left after so much has been lost or stripped away, absorbed in love, dissolved in states of meditation? Much of its identity and sense of self has gone. Yes, there is a past, memories like an old storybook that I can read if I want. But I know that I am just a passerby in this world of time and space, and my ego is not my real self, not my true center of consciousness. It remains a consciousness in this world, with likes and dislikes,[67] but the desires that drew it into life have gone, either fulfilled, fallen away, or destroyed. It also carries some awareness from the states of meditation, just as the dewdrop carries something of the ocean. This "I" has its voice, even if it is just the voice of one who is left behind on the shore. Its light illuminates my life in a particular way.

Compared to the inner world of light, in this world here there is no real clarity, no pure consciousness, but in its shadows and misunderstandings can be found something that belongs to the mystery of life. Certain things can only unfold in the darkness and half-light; certain meanings can only be made known through the veils of misunderstanding. Our ego-consciousness gives meaning to experiences in this world that are hidden from the Self, whose light is too bright, whose consciousness is too direct. And the ego can see a divine quality in life's mysterious interactions, in this interplay of light and dark. It is said that there are possibilities in human experience that are inaccessible to the angels, who only live in the worlds of light.

How can one describe the meaning of these experiences that could be called "mine"? Maybe they are just surface happenings without any deeper significance—an exchange in the post office, a warm cup of tea on a cold morning, a disagreement over nothing of importance. But they are part of this woven web of life that, if one looks closely, contains within it all of creation. They are the little things that make up our days, an e-mail from a friend, the laughter over a silly joke, a memory coming to the surface. But without them life would be stripped of something essential. The Self cannot see these trivialities, cannot know the meaning of the joke, but for the ego they create substance to our life, are part of being alive. This fabric of life contains within it part of the secret of creation that only the ego can see.

In these daily happenings the energy of the earth interacts with our human consciousness. This is part of our story and the story of the soul of the world, forming the web of life that belongs to the sacred meaning of existence. Previous cultures used to honor this in daily rituals and observances. All of life's ordinary occurrences, from planting seeds to baking bread, held a sacred dimension. But in our Western culture we have lost this basic awareness of the sacred. We no longer feel a part of the soul of the world; instead all we are left with are our own individual stories. And too often we feel cut off, isolated, unaware of this underlying connection even though it is all around us.

But even in our individual story is the same pattern of existence, the same myriad of interconnections. My ego-self, no longer caught in desires, can see this web more clearly, see the bigger picture of life into which it is woven. I feel the fabric of life that is all around me, and feel how my own story is part of the world's story. In my feelings, emotions, thoughts, and dreams I experience the subtle colors of this fabric. My own ego is a part of all of this, its story a single thread that is woven into it all. There is only one life—the life of the whole—and yet for each of us it is a different experience. That is part of the mystery of oneness and the magic of creation.

And every day is different, bringing different thoughts or feelings—the play of light and shadows is always slightly different. The ego knows this, lives this, is a vehicle for the uniqueness of this unending change. And there is a fragility to this experience, the fragility of our individual life, here for such a short while, so easily extinguished. This is a part of the beauty of the moment, the brief moment of sunlight being reflected. And even in the midst of life this ego and its story are not "mine," do not belong to me, but are just a spark of sunlight reflected on the waters of life. Light upon light.

On the journey Home so much is given, so much is taken away. And yet I am left with the unexpected sense that after all of the experiences of light and peace and love, after the dark beauty of the uncreated, it is this ordinary story that I will treasure, the happenings of each day, life's dramas and moments of laughter. The ego is so fleeting—I just have to turn inward and it is gone, the dewdrop melted in the sunlight. And yet

only this small self can give me these everyday moments,
the simple story of being human.

8

Where the Two Seas Meet

This chapter explores the questions of the previous chapters, the relationship of human and divine and the mystery and meaning of the "self that remains," in terms of the Sufi figure of Khidr who is found "at the place where the two seas meet," the place where human and divine meet. It looks at the human dimension of what it means to live in this meeting place. What is the nature and purpose of this meeting, and how do we live it?

WHEN I FIRST MET my teacher, Irina Tweedie, I sat in her small room, looked into her blue eyes and I *knew that she knew*. From that moment, without knowing why, more than anything, I wanted what she had. Much later I understood this as the knowledge that can only come from direct inner experience, which for the Sufi is imaged as Khidr. Khidr is the most important Sufi figure, the archetype of direct revelation.

Khidr first appears in the Qur'an where he is not mentioned by name, but as "One of Our servants unto whom We have given mercy from Our Mercy and knowledge from Our Knowledge" (Sūra 18:65). In this story in the Qur'an Khidr is found by Moses at "the place where the two seas meet." This place where the two seas meet is the locus of the mystical journey, "where the dead fish becomes alive," where spiritual teachings become a living substance that nourishes the wayfarer. When we meet our teacher, when we meet the path, this is what happens; something becomes alive within our heart and soul: we become nourished not by spiritual texts or teaching, but by direct transmission.[68] The spiritual journey is a way to live with this spiritual substance, to be burned by its fire, to be consumed by its love.

For many years on the path I longed for this destruction by love, for this transformation so complete that nothing of myself would remain. And I have been given glimpses of a reality where the ego is not present, where there is no "I" to tell its story. And yet in this love story of the soul something has always remained, and gradually I have come to understand a little of the meaning of where this journey takes place, "the place where the two seas meet." It is here, where the divine and human come together, that Khidr is always found. This whole book is an attempt to understand what this means: what it means for the two seas to come together, and what it means to live in this place caught in the currents of the ocean of divine consciousness and yet also held in the sea of human experience.

For so long I struggled to become free of the fetters of existence, of the patterns and problems that bound me to this world of forms. I practiced and meditated, worked with the light and tried to transform my darkness. I was given many experiences of an inner reality where there are no limitations, a landscape which I have called "the further shores of love." Like many wayfarers before me I have been taken, sometimes dragged, beyond myself into the presence of a love that knows no sense of self, that is as it always was. And yet still there is this person trying to tell this story, to make sense of a journey in which I was lost and found and lost again. I am left trying to understand the human dimension of what it means to be where the two seas meet.

Maybe I will only fully understand this story in the moments before physical death, when this human tale is almost over. And yet at this time I am for some reason drawn to understand a little more of this paradox that is my own existence, this mixing place of the two seas. I know that my human consciousness can only understand a little of the Divine, of Its unlimited nature, and the mysterious ways It comes into existence. But I also sense that there is another mystery present in the real nature of myself as a human being, as a part of this limited world of forms, of thoughts, emotions and sensations, and it is this mystery I am trying to comprehend.

The image of the two seas meeting suggests two currents coming together, and such a meeting is never easy, as anyone knows who has been awakened, if just for an instant, to the Divine within himself or herself. There may be a period of grace that is given at the beginning, a time of peace, bliss or inner joy that comes from reconnecting with the Divine. But this is always followed by the turbulence and uncertainty that comes when the two seas meet. This is the inner turmoil the mystic knows so well, when nothing is certain, when the patterns that define our human existence are affected by the more powerful currents from the divine sea, by the vast swells that come from the beyond. We are swept into these seas and then back again into the more inland waters of our human self. Often we need all of our determination to stay above the surface, not to sink gasping for breath. That is why Sufi masters often advise newcomers to keep away from this love—it is dangerous, unpredictable, and destructive. It is not for the fainthearted or those who need the security of a defined world.

For many years the wayfarer is battered by the powerful currents of love's vast ocean, by chaos and confusion, "the dark night, the fear of the waves, the terrifying whirlpool." Often without understanding what is happening, we are surrounded by love in all of its intensity and wonder. This is the love that draws us into the depths, that seems to drown us again and again. And yet always we return to some fragment of self. We come back to the surface, looking for shallower water, a ground that is solid under our feet. And we bring back images of our adventures, dreams of a pearl we have been seeking or an abyss that is always waiting for us to plunge into. These are our stories of the journey, our poems to our self. We try to convince our self that we are not crazy, that this is a planned journey with stages, stations along the way. And yet we know in our belly that nothing is certain except fear and insecurity.

Why can we not just give our self to this love, to this power? Why do we fight, try to defend our self, swim against the current? This too is part of our human drama, the doubts and distress, the anger that can come from deep within. It is not easy to surrender, to give oneself. We are not made in this way. It takes time to bow down before God. And we have to bow down again and again, always when we are most vulnerable. And yet from this battering by love something is born, a silence, a quality of being, a softness that belongs to love's sweetness. There are so many ways the Divine comes alive within us. This inner alchemy is the promise of the heart: that if we stay at the place where the two seas meet we will be changed, that love will reveal its secrets, secrets that are both human and divine.

The divine secrets are in many ways more obvious: experiencing the oneness that belongs to all of life as well as to our relationship with our Beloved, the endlessness of love, its intoxicating bliss, the inner peace it can bring, the compassion. There are many qualities of our divine nature. But what of the human secrets that are revealed? What are we shown about this sea of our self? Yes, there is the ordinariness of life that is given back to us, the simplicity of "chop wood and carry water." Traditionally Khidr appears in the most ordinary form, often over-looked until he has passed: the fisherman we met on the bridge, the child who smiles at us. And in these ordinary moments any image of our self with difficulties or problems disappears and we experience life with a freshness that belongs to the moment; maybe we catch the laughter that is at the core of things. We are more fully alive.

I would like to say that this is all of the story, this return to the simplicity of our self. It has the quality of a return to Eden, recapturing the innocence of a childhood we may have never had. There is no judgment, just pure awareness and often joy. Watching the birds in flight, seeing a leaf fall in the wind, we experience life as fully present. I have been given such moments, which, like a fire in winter, give warmth and light. But what of the person who has made the journey: are all those stories just lost in this sunlight? Does anything remain of the traveler? I have come to believe that even when every image of our self has been dissolved like dew, there is still a story that has a meaning and a purpose. Love's journey brings many scars, often scars in the heart, and they do not all fade away, even if their drama has less-ened. They tell us something about what it means to be human, to stand at the place where the two seas meet, to see the dead fish become alive. And yet, because in moments of real experience there is no time, just the instant that is, these stories do not belong to any past; they are simply a part of what is. They are an essential part of our human mystical experience, our deepest knowing of our self.

For so long I tried to leave myself behind, to abandon it like the wreck of an old car. But always something remained, calling me back. Again and again I tried to avoid it, tried to purify it with love, dissolve it with light. Yet it still remained, as if its story needed to be told, its meaning uncovered. And this is where I am at this moment, with wonder and sadness, knowing that there is part of my own story that is still waiting. It is no longer a story of struggle and transformation, the pain of separation, the bliss of union. And yet it carries the remembrance of these states. It also carries a reminder that we are always separate from our Beloved, always a servant at His feet, even in the presence of the knowing that separation is an illusion and all is one.

So who is this person who is present at this place, whose light is part of the light of God even as I need to live it in my own small life? What really happens when these two seas come together? Do they mix and blend as one, or does each sea retain its own qualities, one speaking of an infinite ocean, the other of an ordinary human experience? How do they come together inside of me, and what story do they tell?

When Moses met Khidr at this place he asked, "Can I follow you, that you may teach me some of the knowledge and the guidance bestowed upon you?" But Khidr said that Moses would not be able to bear being with him, for "How can you stand that which you do not comprehend?" (Sūra 18:68). Three times Moses tried to follow Khidr, until finally he had to leave him, unable to bear his actions. On this journey it appears that the human and divine part ways, and yet the path of the mystic is to bear what we cannot understand, to follow without knowing why. Direct experience cannot be explained to the rational self: we must leave our Moses behind at the water's edge. And yet there is also a human self who makes the journey with Khidr, who does not question or seek to understand. This is the self that remains.

And through this self something is revealed that is hidden from the vaster dimension of our being. It is not just the struggle and confusion, the longing and love, the giving of oneself and attempt at surrender. It is not even the simple awareness of the moment that sees the world with an open eye. Our human self can come to know something about this meeting of the human and divine— a meeting that takes place every moment in every breath, and yet is hidden so quickly by the patterns of existence, by the play of colors and forms we call life. Every moment the Divine comes into existence, and every moment this mystery is hidden the very instant it is revealed. It is quicker than a heartbeat and is so easily overlooked. You can only see it if you are at the place where the two seas meet, where the Divine and human come together. If you look just towards the Divine the light is too bright to see it. And if you are caught in the dramas of being human you will be too slow to notice it.

But every moment this secret is present. It is a moment of divine intention, a spark of divine purpose, that is at the same time our intention and purpose. It is said that we each have a unique, divine purpose, a note of the soul that we alone can play. And this unique note can only be played in this world, in time and space, in the limited world of forms. In the inner worlds that stretch beyond the horizon there is other music, beautiful celestial sounds. But here, in this world, we each have a calling and a purpose, and it seems much of life's journey is to try to live this purpose, play this note. It is the greatest contribution we can make.

In each of us there is a longing to live this purpose, to "find the meaning and make the meaning our goal." This is what calls us on our journey through life, and for some people, if they are fortunate, it is played out through the events of their life, a life which then becomes deeply meaningful and fulfilling. They are living their life's purpose. Of course it is also easy to be sidetracked, caught in the illusions of the world, its pleasures and pain. Then we lose touch with our unique purpose and life becomes gradually more and more meaningless, however we may try to fill it with distractions. For some people spiritual life offers a way to try to regain this meaning, to reconnect with this purpose, and yet it also has its own distractions, illusions of light or "spiritual development." There are so many ways to get lost in this world.

But underneath the play of events, the seeking for meaning and purpose, the losing and finding, is this simple meeting of the Divine and the human: the divine purpose coming into human form. This is what takes place where the two seas meet—this is the meaning of Khidr appearing as an ordinary person. Because one of the greatest mysteries is that there is a divine purpose that is only revealed in this world of forms, and as human beings we carry this purpose in our hearts and in the light of our consciousness. We carry the light of the divine coming into existence, the wave of the divine sea meeting the wave of the human sea. We are the divine purpose being made manifest. This is the hidden love story of the world, which the Sufis call the secret of the word "*Kun!*" ("Be!").

All of the struggle and seeking for meaning takes one to this place, to this meeting that happens again and again in every instant. The currents of the Divine come to meet us and we come to meet the Divine. And in that meeting we merge and are one, as two waves coming together, and yet also remain separate—because as Ibn 'Arabī reminds us, "the servant is always the servant and the Lord is always the Lord." This is the promise and the pain of the mystic: we long to return to love's infinite ocean, to merge back into the source. And yet we have to remain here in this physical world of multiplicity to play the unique note of our being. We have to honor what it means to be a human being even if we have tasted what it means to be dissolved in love.

My journey has brought me to live where the two seas meet. I know the nothingness, the primal emptiness that is within every atom and every breath. I know the bliss of absorption and what it means to be drawn into "the dark silence in which all lovers lose themselves." And I also know the pain of returning, of accepting the limitations of my own everyday self, the simple joys and pain of being human, the everyday dramas we all enact. But it seems that my story is to hold these seeming opposites. I remember a line I wrote soon after I first came to the path almost forty years ago: "I am caught in the coils of infinity, and yet held in the presence of time." This has always been part of my journey, part of the meaning I have been asked to live. Now, after so many years, I understand it a little more. Hopefully I have learned to accept it.

Here, where the two seas meet, I find a light that holds my attention. It is a light that holds an intention, a purpose that cannot be defined but is. To be at the place where the two seas meet means for me to hold this light, to embody this intention. This intention has a purity that belongs to the beyond, a purpose that belongs to my Beloved. And it is held in the heart, a heart that knows suffering and surrender, that beats with the blood of life and also carries the consciousness of the Divine. This for me is where meaning is born, where the story I call my life continues to unfold.

Once you have tasted the ocean of love's oneness it is in your blood. It is always calling to you, sometimes from afar and sometimes so close you can feel its presence. It is like a lover you always long for. It is then so easy to be lost in love, dissolved in light. To remain is not so easy. Sometimes it tears the heart. Yet only in the moment of human experience, between the in-breath and the out-breath, is that light of meaning made manifest. And this light coming into the world, being manifest in each of us, is the love story of the Beloved. For me to live this love story is to be present where the two seas meet, to hold this tension, this paradox. Here, in this meeting of the infinite ocean of divine love with the frailty of my human self, in my own heart and mind and body, His love story is being told—told to me, for me, and through me. And what can I continue to do with my life but live this love story of my Beloved? The fragment of my own self that remains is just a fragment of His love story—that is all it ever is. Just a fragment of a love story.

The Beloved gave me some dust from the backyard.
Why are you so fragrant, oh, dust?
I am a dust people tread upon,
But I partake of the fragrance of the courtyard of a Saint.
It is not me, I am just an ordinary dust.
So if people praise you,
you must say that you were just near a flower,
but you are an ordinary dust.
And it is all due to His Lotus feet.[69]

Persian Poem

Notes

OPENING & INTRODUCTION

1. *Divine Flashes*, trans. William Chittick and Peter Lamborn Wilson, p. 111.
2. I use the term "God" not in reference to an anthropomorphic father figure, but to an all-pervading, ever-present Reality that is both immanent ("closer to him than his neck vein," Qur'an 50:16) and transcendent ("beyond even our idea of the beyond"). Sufis call this Reality the "Beloved."
3. The Zen saying:

   > The wild geese do not intend to cast their reflection,
   > The water has no mind to receive their image.

4. See *The Face Before I Was Born: A Spiritual Autobiography*, second edition 2009, published by The Golden Sufi Center.
5. Fakhruddīn 'Irāqī, *Divine Flashes*, p. 99.

1. DUST AT HIS FEET

6. Quoted by Mohammad Shafii, *Freedom from the Self*, p. 45. Other Sufis make similar statements about the need for a teacher at the very beginning of the journey:

   Abū'l-Hasan 'Ali al-Kharaqānī states:

   > In the beginning you must do two things. One is journeying and the other is you must take a master.

   Quoted by Abū Sa'īd ibn Abī'l-Khayr, *The Secret of God's Mystical Oneness*, trans. John O'Kane, p. 120.

   And Rūmī says:

   > Choose a master, for without him this journey is full of tribulations, fears and dangers. With no escort, you would be lost on a road you would have already taken. Do not travel alone on the Path.

   Mathnawī, I, 2943-45, quoted by Eva de Vitray-Meyerovitch in *Rūmī and Sufism*, p. 117.

7. Irina Tweedie had been trained by her sheikh, Bhai Sahib, so that after he died she could contact him when she was in meditation. She describes her first experience of this one

night in the Himalayas, "Now only a tremendous Power to be reached in moments of non-being... a center of blissful energy, an answer to my cry for help... How could I even think in the past that he deceived me? That I was left an orphan, that I would never reach him? He showed me the way to reach him through the divine love." *Daughter of Fire*, p. 794.

8. I refer to Irina Tweedie, or Mrs. Tweedie as she liked to be known, as my teacher as she is the one who outwardly guided me for so many years, and I still experience her inner guidance and help with the work. But her sheikh, the Sufi master Radha Mohan Lal whom she refers to as Bhai Sahib (elder brother), is my sheikh, with whom I have an ancient connection of the soul, from lifetime to lifetime. Although I have never known him in the physical world, he is the one to whom I belong beyond life and death. He is always with me. In Sufism a connection with a master that exists solely on the spiritual plane is called *Uwaysī*. It belongs especially to the Naqshbandi *tariqa*.

9. *Daughter of Fire*, p. 275.

10. Ibid. p. 496.

2. CHAMBERS OF THE HEART

11. *A Treatise on the Heart*, trans. Nicholas Heer, *Three Early Sufi Texts*, p. 45.

12. Naqshbandi saying. "The Journey Home" is the third of the Eleven Naqshbandi Principles. See: www.goldensufi.org/eleven_principles.html.

13. Al-Jīlānī, *The Secret of Secrets*, ed. Tosun Bayrak, p. 15.

14. Different Sufi manuals describe different numbers of the heart's *latāif*: four, five, six, and even seven. Sufi teachers developed specific techniques for accessing the different *latāif*, using *dhikr*, breathing practices, and visualizations. The different *latāif* were also associated with different parts of the body.

15. Quoted by Irina Tweedie, *Daughter of Fire*, p. 87.

16. Trans. Vraje Abramian, unpublished.

17. Rūmī, *Light upon Light,* trans. Andrew Harvey, p. 103.

18. Quoted by Annemarie Schimmel, *As Through a Veil*, p. 32.

19. Quoted by Henry Corbin, *The Man of Light in Iranian Sufism*, p. 72.

20. *Daughter of Fire*, p. 79.
21. Fakhruddīn 'Irāqī, quoted in *Divine Flashes*, trans. William Chittick and Peter Lamborn Wilson, p. 111.
22. Quoted by Massignon, *The Passion of al-Hallāj*, vol. 3, p. 47.
23. Farīd al-Dīn 'Attār, trans. Hellmut Ritter and John O'Kane, *The Ocean of the Soul*, p. 555.
24. Some Sufis say that in order to be taken into this chamber of the heart, in order to make the transition from a world of duality to the mystery of divine oneness, you need to be given a substance that they call *Sirr*. This substance is given through the grace of the sheikh and through the mystery of spiritual transmission, infused from heart to heart.
25. Quoted by Massignon, *The Passion of al-Hallāj*, vol. 3, p. 42.
26. Sa'd al-Dīn Hamawī, *Love's Alchemy: Poems from the Sufi Tradition*, trans. David and Sabrineh Fideler, p. 127.
27. Qur'an 2:115.
28. Mīr Dard, quoted by Schimmel, *Mystical Dimensions of Islam*, p. 289.
29. *Hadīth qudsī*.
30. 'Ayn'l-Qudāt Hamadhānī, quoted by Hellmut Ritter, *The Ocean of the Soul*, p. 493.
31. Quoted by Massignon, *The Passion of al-Hallāj*, vol 3, p. 42.
32. This is similar to the non-dual contemplation of the Buddhists:

    "To see directly the absolute state, the Ground of our being, is the View…. It is nothing less than *seeing* the actual state of things as they are; it is *knowing* that the true nature of mind is the true nature of everything…"

    Sögyal Rinpoche, *The Tibetan Book of Living and Dying*, p. 156.
33. *Abdullah Ansari of Herat*, trans. A. G. Ravan Farhādi, p. 110.
34. Rūmī, *Light upon Light*, trans. Andrew Harvey, p. 173.
35. *The Ocean of the Soul*, trans. Hellmut Ritter and John O'Kane, p. 605.
36. Irina Tweedie, *Daughter of Fire*, p. 728.
37. Farīd al-Dīn 'Attār, *The Ocean of the Soul*, trans. Hellmut Ritter and John O'Kane, p. 612.

38. See footnote 8 above for the difference between my relation-ship with my teacher, Irina Tweedie, and my sheikh, Radha Mohan Lal.

39. In a dream I had soon after I began this work, a voice said, "I am hung in the house of God."

40. *St. John* 20:16.

41. The teacher is like a "ferryman." Bahā ud-Dīn Naqshband said: "We are the means of reaching the goal. It is necessary that seekers should cut themselves away from us and think only of the goal." Quoted by J. G. Bennett, *Masters of Wisdom*, p. 140.

42. Traditionally "the teacher finds the disciple," and over these years of traveling in America through giving lectures and workshops I met those individuals who had an inner connec-tion to this Sufi path. Sensing this connection these individuals would come and speak to me during or after the event about how to follow this path more deeply. Now that the path is more visible, people are attracted to this path through books, articles, and the Internet.

43. There are also groups in other parts of the world, South Africa, Australia, Argentina, as well as individuals following this path scattered in different countries.

44. It is important to differentiate between a religion with its exoteric teachings and doctrine, and a spiritual tradition which has an esoteric, inner dimension. America has a constitutional respect for religious freedom but little understanding or appreciation of spiritual traditions, their disciplines and practices, and the importance of inner work rather than any code of belief.

45. Irina Tweedie, *Daughter of Fire*, p. 58.

46. Ibid. p. 718.

47. During this time I went on a lecture trip to Australia, and when I arrived I was shocked to find that the cloud that had covered my spiritual work was no longer there; suddenly there was clear sunshine and bright light. For the first time in years I felt a deep joy and lightness again present. Flying back to America once again I experienced the clouds covering the spiritual sun.

48. For further information on the relationship between individual spiritual practice and global transformation, and the role of spiritual awareness in helping the world evolve, see *Awakening the World: A Global Dimension to Spiritual Practice* by Llewellyn Vaughan-Lee.

5. WHO MAKES THE JOURNEY?

49. *The Ocean of the Soul*, trans. Hellmut Ritter, p. 493.
50. Farīd al-Dīn 'Attār, *The Conference of the Birds*, trans. Afkham Darbandi and Dick Davis, p. 219.
51. Ibid. p. 219-220.
52. Ibid. p. 229.
53. *The Drunken Universe*, p. 96.
54. Mīr Dard, quoted by Annemarie Schimmel, *Pain and Grace*. p. 193.
55. Fakhruddīn 'Irāqī, *The Ocean of the Soul*, trans. Hellmut Ritter, p. 498.
56. Fakhruddīn 'Irāqī, *Divine Flashes*, p. 120.
57. Quoted by William Chittick, *The Sufi Path of Knowledge*, p. 365.

7. MEDITATION AND THE "I"

58. *Divine Flashes*, p. 127.
59. The I who is recounting this is not the ego, but the witness (*shāhid*) or observing self, that has a quality of detachment that comes from the Self.
60. Psychologically the ego is no longer the center of consciousness, but takes its place as part of the mandala of the Self.
61. *The Life, Personality and Writings of Al-Junayd*, trans. Abdel-Kader, p. 90. See Vaughan-Lee, *The Circle of Love*, pp. 141-152 for a fuller exploration of this state.
62. "To be present and absent at the same time means a continual strain on the self." *The Life, Personality and Writings of Al-Junayd*, trans. Abdel-Kader, p. 91.
63. This state is sometimes called "The Second Separation." To quote Junayd "After their union with Him, He separates them from Him (and grants them their individuality again)." *The Life, Personality and Writings of Al-Junayd*, trans. Abdel-Kader, p. 90.

64. I should note that this does not always happen, that there are meditations when the mind and the ego are still present with concerns and thoughts, but there is always the sense that behind their activity is a deeper, vaster presence.

65. There are energies that belong to the physical world and its elemental forces which are a part of our incarnation. For example, one's "power animal" is an inner energy directly related to the animal kingdom.

66. It is this light within the ego that attracts us to the experiences the soul needs, though of course we are also caught in the lower desires of the ego, in its shadow, conditioning and other dynamics. Life's maze can lead us to the center of our self or lose us.

67. I still like Swiss chocolate and cheese, walking in the early morning, listening to Bach and Mozart. I dislike crowds and the telephone.

8. WHERE THE TWO SEAS MEET

68. The most celebrated example of this is Rūmī's meeting with Shams, when the theology professor left behind his books to become one of the world's most loved mystics.

CLOSING PAGE

69. Persian poem, quoted by Irina Tweedie in *Daughter of Fire*, p. 496.

Index

Bibliography

'Aṭṭār, Farīd al-Dīn. *The Ocean of the Soul*. Trans. Hellmut Ritter and John O'Kane. Boston: Brill, 2003.

— *The Conference of the Birds*. Trans. Afkham Darbandi and Dick Davis. London: Penguin, 1984.

Abū Saʿīd ibn Abī'l-Khayr. *The Secret of God's Mystical Oneness*. Trans. John O'Kane. Costa Mesa, CA: Mazda Publishers, 1992.

Bennett, J. G. *The Masters of Wisdom*. London: Turnstone Press, 1977.

Chittick, William C. *The Sufi Path of Knowledge*. Albany: State University of New York Press, 1989.

Corbin, Henry. *The Man of Light in Iranian Sufism.* London: Shambhala Publications, 1978.

Fakhruddīn 'Irāqī. *Divine Flashes*. Trans. William C. Chittick and Peter Lamborn Wilson. New York: Paulist Press, 1982.

Fideler, David and Sabrineh, *Love's Alchemy*. Novato, CA: New World Library, 2006.

Heer, Nicholas, ed. *Three Early Sufi Texts*. Louisville: Fons Vitae, 2003.

Jīlānī, al-, *The Secret of Secrets*. Interpreted Tosun Bayrak al-Jerrahi al-Halveti. Cambridge: Islamic Texts Society, 1992.

Junayd, al-, *The Life, Personality and Writings of Al-Junayd*. Trans. Ali Hassan Abdel-Kader. London: Luzac & Co, 1976.

Massignon, Louis. *The Passion of al-Hallāj*. Princeton: Princeton University Press, 1982.

Shafii, Mohammad, *Freedom from the Self*. New York: Human Sciences Press, 1985.

Rūmī. *Light Upon Light*. Trans. Andrew Harvey. Berkeley: North Atlantic Books, 1996.

Schimmel, Annemarie. *Mystical Dimensions of Islam*. Chapel Hill: University of North Carolina Press, 1975.

— *Pain and Grace*. Leiden: E. J. Brill, 1976.

Tweedie, Irina. *Daughter of Fire: A Diary of a Spiritual Training with a Sufi Master*. Point Reyes, CA: The Golden Sufi Center, 1986.

Vitray-Meyerovitch, Eva de. *Rūmī and Sufism*. Sausalito, CA: The Post-Apollo Press, 1987.

Acknowledgments

For permission to use copyrighted material, the author gratefully wishes to acknowledge: Paulist Press for excerpts from *Fakhruddin Iraqi: Divine Flashes*, from The Classics of Western Spirituality Series, translated with an introduction by William Chittick and Peter Wilson, Copyright © 1982, 2011 by Paulist Press, Inc., New York/Mahwah, NJ and used with permission of Paulist Press, www.paulistpress.com; David and Sabrineh Fideler for excerpt from *Love's Alchemy: Poems from the Sufi Tradition*, translated by David and Sabrineh Fideler, copyright © 2006 by David and Sabrineh Fideler, published by New World Library; Brill Academic Publishers for excerpts from *The Ocean of the Soul: Man, the World, and God in the Stories of Farid al-Din Attar*, by Hellmut Ritter, translated by John O'Kane with assistance from Bernd Radtke, copyright © 2003 Koninklijke Brill, NV, Leiden, The Netherlands, published by Brill Academic Publishers; and Penguin Books Ltd., for permission to quote twelve lines (pp. 219, 220, 229) from *The Conference of the Birds* by Farīd ud-Dīn Attār, translated by Afkham Darbandi and Dick Davis, copyright © 1984 Afkham Darbandi and Dick Davis, published by Penguin Classics.

About the Author

LLEWELLYN VAUGHAN-LEE, Ph.D., is a Sufi teacher in the Naqshbandiyya-Mujaddidiyya Sufi Order. Born in London in 1953, he has followed the Naqshbandi Sufi path since he was nineteen. In 1991 he became the successor of Irina Tweedie, author of *Daughter of Fire: A Diary of a Spiritual Training with a Sufi Master*. He then moved to Northern California and founded The Golden Sufi Center (www.goldensufi.org). Author of several books, he has specialized in the area of dreamwork, integrating the ancient Sufi approach to dreams with the insights of Jungian Psychology. Since 2000 the focus of his writing and teaching has been on spiritual responsibility in our present time of transition, and an awakening global consciousness of oneness. More recently he has written about the feminine, the *Anima Mundi* (world soul), and spiritual ecology (see www.workingwithoneness.org).

About the Publisher

THE GOLDEN SUFI CENTER publishes books, video, and audio on Sufism and mysticism. A California religious nonprofit 501 (c) (3) corporation, it is dedicated to making the teachings of the Naqshbandi Sufi path available to all seekers. For further information about the activities and publications, please contact:

THE GOLDEN SUFI CENTER
P.O. Box 456
Point Reyes Station, CA 94956-0456
tel: 415-663-0100 · fax: 415-663-0103
www.goldensufi.org

The Golden Sufi Center® Publications
www.goldensufi.org/books.html

by IRINA TWEEDIE

DAUGHTER OF FIRE:
A Diary of a Spiritual Training with a Sufi Master

~

by LLEWELLYN VAUGHAN-LEE

THE RETURN OF THE FEMININE AND THE WORLD SOUL

ALCHEMY OF LIGHT:
Working with the Primal Energies of Life

AWAKENING THE WORLD:
A Global Dimension to Spiritual Practice

SPIRITUAL POWER: *How It Works*

MOSHKEL GOSHA:
A Story of Transformation

LIGHT OF ONENESS

WORKING WITH ONENESS

THE SIGNS OF GOD

LOVE IS A FIRE:
The Sufi's Mystical Journey Home

THE CIRCLE OF LOVE

CATCHING THE THREAD:
Sufism, Dreamwork, and Jungian Psychology

THE FACE BEFORE I WAS BORN:
A Spiritual Autobiography

THE PARADOXES OF LOVE

Sufism, the Transformation of the Heart

In the Company of Friends:
Dreamwork within a Sufi Group

The Bond with the Beloved:
The Mystical Relationship of the Lover and the Beloved

⁓

edited by LLEWELLYN VAUGHAN-LEE
with biographical information by SARA SVIRI

Travelling the Path of Love:
Sayings of Sufi Masters

⁓

by PETER KINGSLEY

A Story Waiting to Pierce You:
Mongolia, Tibet and the Destiny of the Western World

Reality

In the Dark Places of Wisdom

⁓

by SARA SVIRI

The Taste of Hidden Things:
Images of the Sufi Path

⁓

by HILARY HART

The Unknown She:
Eight Faces of an Emerging Consciousness

⁓